PREFACE

1. Scope

This publication provides doctrine for cross-functional geospatial intelligence (GEOINT) support to joint operations. It discusses roles, GEOINT operational processes, planning, coordination, production, dissemination, existing architectures, and assessment of GEOINT.

2. Purpose

This publication has been prepared under the direction of the Chairman of the Joint Chiefs of Staff. It sets forth joint doctrine to govern the activities and performance of the Armed Forces of the United States in joint operations, and provides the doctrinal basis for interagency coordination and for US military involvement in multinational operations. It provides military guidance for the exercise of authority by combatant commanders and other joint force commanders (JFCs) and prescribes joint doctrine for operations, education, and training. It provides military guidance for use by the Armed Forces in preparing their appropriate plans. It is not the intent of this publication to restrict the authority of the JFC from organizing the force and executing the mission in a manner the JFC deems most appropriate to ensure unity of effort in the accomplishment of the overall objective.

3. Application

a. Joint doctrine established in this publication applies to the Joint Staff, commanders of combatant commands, subunified commands, joint task forces, subordinate components of these commands, combat support agencies, and the Services.

b. The guidance in this publication is authoritative; as such, this doctrine will be followed except when, in the judgment of the commander, exceptional circumstances dictate otherwise. If conflicts arise between the contents of this publication and the contents of Service publications, this publication will take precedence unless the Chairman of the Joint Chiefs of Staff, normally in coordination with the other members of the Joint Chiefs of Staff, has provided more current and specific guidance. Commanders of forces operating as part of a multinational (alliance or coalition) military command should follow multinational doctrine and procedures ratified by the US. For doctrine and procedures not ratified by the US, commanders should evaluate and follow the multinational command's doctrine and procedures, where applicable and consistent with US law, regulations, and doctrine.

For the Chairman of the Joint Chiefs of Staff:

CURTIS M. SCAPARROTTI
Lieutenant General, U.S. Army
Director, Joint Staff

Intentionally Blank

SUMMARY OF CHANGES
REVISION OF JOINT PUBLICATION 2-03
DATED 22 MARCH 2007

- Modifies the construct of geospatial intelligence (GEOINT), which may consist of imagery, imagery intelligence, and geospatial information.

- Adds Safety of Navigation reference of Global Positioning System (GPS) as the primary source of positioning, navigation, and timing information and describes the significance GPS plays in GEOINT information.

- Deletes reference to the Defense Intelligence Operations Coordination Center (DIOCC). DIOCC disestablishment occurred on 1 October 2011.

- Updates the support activities of US Strategic Command.

- Adds US Transportation Command's Unified Command Plan (UCP) responsibility for synchronizing planning for global distribution operations.

- Revises the US Transportation Command's subordinate command to include the Joint Enabling Capabilities Command.

- Updates US Special Operations Command's responsibilities based on UCP change.

- Provides an expanded summary of US Air Force support to GEOINT.

- Modifies wording of the US Coast Guard's surveillance mission.

- Includes features associated with cyberspace.

- Modifies phases of imagery exploitation.

- Replaces current remote replication services with former remote GEOINT services.

- Modifies GEOINT targeting support.

- Clarifies real-time meteorological and oceanographic (METOC) support and data.

- Updates Navy METOC center web pages and links.

Intentionally Blank

TABLE OF CONTENTS

APPENDIX

GLOSSARY

FIGURE

EXECUTIVE SUMMARY
COMMANDER'S OVERVIEW

- **Provides an Overview of Geospatial Intelligence (GEOINT) in Joint Operations**

- **Explains the Roles and Responsibilities for GEOINT**

- **Describes the Joint Operations Context for GEOINT**

- **Covers the GEOINT Operations Process**

Geospatial Intelligence in Joint Operations

Geospatial Intelligence (GEOINT) is the exploitation and analysis of imagery and geospatial information to describe, assess, and visually depict physical features and geographically referenced activities on the Earth.

Joint forces require the ability to rapidly respond to threats around the world. Geospatial intelligence (GEOINT) supports this requirement by providing geo-referenced visual and data products (e.g., maps, charts, digital file, imagery, and digital raster or vector information) that serve as a foundation and common frame of reference for any joint operation.

GEOINT operations are the tasks, activities, and events to collect, manage, analyze, generate, visualize, and provide imagery, imagery intelligence, and geospatial information necessary to support national and defense missions and international arrangements.

Advances in technology and the use of geospatial data throughout the joint force have created the ability to use geography by integrating more sophisticated capabilities for visualization, analysis, and dissemination of fused views of the operational environment. This capability provides many advantages for the warfighter, national security policymakers, homeland security personnel, and intelligence community (IC) collaborators by precisely locating activities and objects, enabling safe navigation over air, land, and sea, assessing and discerning the meaning of events, and providing context for decision makers.

Roles and Responsibilities

National and Department of Defense-Level Entities

The National System for Geospatial Intelligence (NSG) is the combination of technology, policies, capabilities, doctrine, activities, people, data, and organizations necessary to produce GEOINT in an integrated, multi-intelligence environment.

The NSG community consists of members of the IC, Services, Joint Staff, combatant command (CCMDs), Civil Applications Committee members, international partners, industry, academia, and defense and civil community service providers.

National Geospatial-Intelligence Agency.

By law, National Geospatial-Intelligence Agency (NGA) is a combat support agency as well as a national intelligence organization, and is directly subordinate to Secretary of Defense and the Under Secretary of Defense for Intelligence. NGA is the primary source for GEOINT analysis, products, data and services at the national level.

National Reconnaissance Office

The National Reconnaissance Office designs, builds, and operates the nation's reconnaissance satellites, which comprise one of the primary collection sources for GEOINT data. Once GEOINT data is collected, processed, and stored, NGA takes the lead with analysis and access/distribution for both national and Department of Defense (DOD) customers.

Joint Staff

The Joint Staff Intelligence Directorate of a Joint staff (J-2) is responsible for GEOINT policy and procedures. The Joint Staff J-2 GEOINT officer interacts with NGA, the Services, and CCMDs to help articulate, refine, and prioritize GEOINT requirements.

Combatant Commands

The CCMDs develop GEOINT area and point target requirements to support indications and warning as well as the planning and execution of joint operations.

Subordinate Joint Force Commander

Like the combatant commanders (CCDRs), subordinate joint force commanders develop area and point target GEOINT requirements to support the planning and execution of joint operations.

Services

The Services support their departmental planning functions and CCMDs with GEOINT products, Service-specific content, format, and media. Designated Service geospatial information and services (GI&S) functional managers are responsible for coordinating with the CCMD's joint intelligence operations center (JIOC) and NGA to establish policy regarding roles and responsibilities for co-production, value adding, and management of distributed geospatial libraries.

Non-Department of Defense Agencies

While US DOD and IC agencies are key GEOINT producers, civil agencies are playing an increasing role supporting operations, whether they are military or humanitarian in nature. As examples, the Department of Interior's United States Geological Survey and elements of the Department of Homeland Defense participate with the NSG in providing support to defense and civil operations through the acquisition and analysis of commercial imagery and topographic products.

Commonwealth Partners

As functional manager of GEOINT and the NSG, the Director of National Geospatial-Intelligence Agency strives to incorporate to the maximum extent its four primary commonwealth partners—Australia, Canada, and the United Kingdom. These countries work closely with the US theater CCMD's JIOC on GEOINT production as part of the unified GEOINT operations.

Joint Operations Context for Geospatial Intelligence

Command Joint Intelligence Operations Center

The JIOC is the focal point for the CCMD's intelligence planning, collection management, analysis, and production effort, and is organized to satisfy the CCDR's intelligence requirements. NGA provides direct support to each of the CCMD JIOCs.

Joint GEOINT Cell

The CCMD GEOINT cell is responsible for coordinating all GEOINT requirements within its area of responsibility while ensuring that the supporting commands or component commands are managing theater and mission-specific GEOINT requirements. The GEOINT cell facilitates the use of standardized GEOINT processes, procedures, and organizations across the CCMDs,

Joint Intelligence Preparation of the Operational Environment

Subordinate commands should utilize compatible GEOINT products, data, and standards to facilitate joint intelligence preparation of the operational environment (JIPOE) processes and products developed by the joint force J-2 to adequately support the mission. GEOINT analysts generally support the entire JIPOE process, but specifically **Step 2, describes the impact of the operational environment.** During this step, analysts evaluate the impact of the operational environment on adversary, friendly, and neutral military capabilities and broad courses of action. All relevant physical and nonphysical aspects of the operational environment are analyzed to produce a geospatial perspective.

Geospatial Intelligence Operations Process

The GEOINT operations process builds upon the intelligence process; tasking, processing, exploitation, and dissemination capabilities; and joint warfighter interoperable GEOINT process models.

The GEOINT operations process is described by a set of interrelated and specific activities and procedures that provide situational awareness and support operations. These activities and subtasks are continuous and may be performed independently, in conjunction with one another, or as a component of other intelligence or operational procedures that require information fusion, visualization, analysis, and sharing. **The GEOINT operations process activities are: direction, planning, and requirements management; discover and obtain geospatial intelligence; task and collection; processing and exploitation; analysis, production, and visualization; value-added; and dissemination, sharing, and storage.**

Direction, Planning, and Requirements Management

The GEOINT cell will develop and publish CCMD GEOINT concept of operations to delineate management of the GEOINT cell and the GEOINT operations process for coordination and collaboration within the CCMD operational processes to maximize the efficiency of GEOINT capabilities. The GEOINT cell conducts planning for GEOINT-related needs and operational activities of the CCMD and joint task forces (JTFs). The GEOINT cell coordinates across all functions of the command and subordinate commands to identify and prioritize joint GEOINT mission requirements to enable fusion, visualization, analysis, and sharing based upon the assigned mission. GEOINT requirements include the data, information, and product needs for GI&S and imagery to support weapons systems, JTF operations, command and control, and intelligence functions.

Discover and Obtain GEOINT

The GEOINT cell coordinates the procedures and manages the tasks to search for, find, access, and gather GEOINT information and data from existing holdings, databases, and libraries. The user can manipulate data from available libraries or databases to create tailored products or data sets for specific mission purposes or military applications.

Tasking and Collection

Tasking involves expressing GEOINT needs in the form of collection requirements to appropriate collection assets to acquire data or information necessary to meet mission objectives. Requirements flow through a variety of tasking systems such as GI&S, imagery, intelligence, and other information channels. Collection includes those activities related to the acquisition of GEOINT data or information required to satisfy tasked requirements.

Processing and Exploitation

GEOINT processing may include automated, semi-automated, and manual procedures to integrate or conflate data. After being processed, GEOINT is distributed, archived, and made accessible for users. Exploitation involves the evaluation and manipulation of GEOINT data to extract information related to a list of essential elements of information. Exploitation results in the extraction of information and data that is specifically selected for use or integration in subsequent tasks in the GEOINT operations process.

Analysis, Production, and Visualization

Once data has been processed, it can be used as source to and produce either general intelligence and describe, assess, or visually depict information in standard or tailored GEOINT products. The GEOINT cell coordinates the use, interpretation, and integration of information into intelligence, standard or tailored products and data, and visual presentations of situational awareness, and trend analysis in response to expressed or anticipated requirements and information needs.

Value-Added

Value adding may include, but is not limited to, data verification, correction, update, densification, supplementation with additional categories of content, reformatting, seismic activity, orthorectification, map finishing and three-dimensional visualization, and intelligence reports. Enhancing GEOINT consists of operations performed on a foundation of existing GEOINT content that increases its value for subsequent use.

Dissemination, Sharing, and Storage

Dissemination is accomplished through both the "pull" and "push" principles. The pull principle provides intelligence organizations at all levels with direct reachback capability via electronic access to central databases, intelligence files, or other repositories containing GEOINT data and products, as well as to services from other entities. The push principle allows the producers to transmit GEOINT, along with other relevant information, to those who have registered standing interest in certain regions, products, or types of content.

CONCLUSION

This publication provides doctrine for cross-functional GEOINT support to joint operations. It discusses roles, GEOINT operational processes, planning, coordination, production, dissemination, existing architectures, and assessment of GEOINT.

CHAPTER I
GEOSPATIAL INTELLIGENCE IN JOINT OPERATIONS

> *"The want of accurate maps of the Country which has hitherto been the Scene of War, has been a great disadvantage to me. I have in vain endeavored to procure them and have been obliged to make shift with such sketches as I could trace from my own Observations..."*
>
> **The words of General George Washington, according to John C. Fitzpatrick,**
> ***Writings of George Washington from the Original Manuscript Sources,***
> **1745-1799, ed. (Washington, D.C.: Government Printing Office, 1931-44)**

1. Introduction

a. Joint forces require the ability to rapidly respond to threats around the world. Geospatial intelligence (GEOINT) supports this requirement by providing geo-referenced visual and data products (e.g., maps, charts, digital file, imagery, and digital raster or vector information) that serve as a foundation and common frame of reference for any joint operation.

b. GEOINT is defined in Title 10, United States Code (USC), Section 467, as "the exploitation and analysis of imagery and geospatial information to describe, assess, and visually depict physical features and geographically referenced activities on the Earth. GEOINT consists of imagery, imagery intelligence (IMINT), and geospatial information." Any one or combination of these three elements may be considered GEOINT.

c. The National Geospatial-Intelligence Agency (NGA) mission to provide GEOINT is established in Title 10, USC, Section 442 and Title 50, USC, Section 404e.

2. Geospatial Intelligence Overview

a. GEOINT is an intelligence discipline that has evolved from the integration of imagery, IMINT, and geospatial information to a broader cross-functional effort in support of national and defense missions and international arrangements. Advances in technology and the use of geospatial data throughout the joint force have created the ability to use geography by integrating more sophisticated capabilities for visualization, analysis, and dissemination of fused views of the operational environment. The full utility of GEOINT comes from the integration of all three, which results in more comprehensive, tailored GEOINT products for a wider scope of problems and customers across all functional areas. This capability provides many advantages for the warfighter, national security policymakers, homeland security personnel, and intelligence community (IC) collaborators by precisely locating activities and objects, enabling safe navigation over air, land, and sea, assessing and discerning the meaning of events, and providing context for decision makers.

b. GEOINT operations are the tasks, activities, and events to collect, manage, analyze, generate, visualize, and provide imagery, IMINT, and geospatial information necessary to support national and defense missions and international arrangements. GEOINT operations are comprised of a set of interrelated and specific activities and procedures to conduct GEOINT and cross-functional operational awareness of the environment. These activities continuously support information fusion, visualization, analysis, and sharing. They may be performed independently, in conjunction with one another, or as a component of other intelligence or information-related activities. GEOINT operations include the collection of information for extraction, storage, dissemination, and exploitation of geographic, geodetic, geomagnetic, imagery, gravimetric, aeronautical, topographic, hydrographic, littoral, cultural, and toponymic, and any other data referenced to a location on, above, or below the Earth. These data sets are used for military planning, training and operations, including navigation, mission planning, mission rehearsal modeling and simulation, and precise geolocation supporting targeting. GEOINT provides the basic framework for visualizing the operational environment. It is information produced by multiple sources to common interoperable data standards. GEOINT supports the common operational picture (COP). It may be presented in the form of printed maps, charts, digital files, and publications; in digital simulation and modeling databases; in web enabled databases; in photographic form; or in the form of digitized maps and charts or attributed data. GEOINT services include tools that enable users to access and manipulate data and also include instruction, training, laboratory support, weapon systems analysis, and guidance for the use of geospatial data. The base geospatial information which provides the underlying data to provide context and a framework for display and visualization of the environment to support analysis operations and intelligence is called foundation GEOINT, and consists of the following: features, elevation, controlled imagery, geodetic sciences, geographic names and boundaries, aeronautical, maritime, and human geography.

3. Geospatial Intelligence Support to Joint Operations

a. GEOINT provides a common framework for supporting joint operations to better enable mission accomplishment across the range of military operations and with all mission partners. GEOINT supports joint operations through the multidirectional flow and integration of geospatially (i.e., spatiotemporally)-referenced data from relevant GEOINT and multi-intelligence sources to achieve shared awareness of the operational environment, near-real-time tracking, and collaboration between forces. GEOINT capabilities are crucial to developing a context of space and time regarding the operational environment for the creation of knowledge about trends and patterns for operational awareness and decision making. GEOINT activities should be coordinated within a GEOINT cell under the staff organization structure of the joint force command.

b. GEOINT operations activities necessary to support joint operations include the capability to direct, plan, and manage GEOINT requirements; discover and retrieve GEOINT; task and collect GEOINT; analyze, produce, and visualize GEOINT; add value to GEOINT; and disseminate, share, and store GEOINT. The GEOINT cell interacts directly with customers and the National System for Geospatial Intelligence (NSG) to obtain and provide the best quality GEOINT possible in response to validated mission requirements. The GEOINT operations process is described by a set of seven interrelated and specific activities and procedures to conduct GEOINT and support situational awareness (SA). These activities, described below, are continuous and may be performed independently, in

---

GEOSPATIAL INTELLIGENCE ELEMENTS

Imagery: A likeness or presentation of any natural or man-made feature or related object or activity and the positional data acquired at the same time the likeness or representation was acquired, including products produced by space-based national intelligence reconnaissance systems, and likenesses or presentations produced by satellites, airborne platforms, unmanned aerial vehicles, or other similar means (except that such term does not include handheld or clandestine photography taken by or on behalf of human intelligence collection organizations).

Imagery Intelligence: The technical, geographic, and intelligence information derived through the interpretation or analysis of imagery and collateral materials.

Geospatial Information: Information that identifies the geographic location and characteristics of natural or constructed features and boundaries on the Earth, including: statistical data and information derived from, among other things, remote sensing, mapping, and surveying technologies; and mapping, charting, geodetic data, and related products.

SOURCE: Definitions from Title 10, United States Code, Section 467

---

conjunction with one another, or integrated as a component of other intelligence disciplines or operational procedures that require information fusion, visualization, analysis, and sharing. Although similar to the intelligence process, the GEOINT operations process builds upon the cross-functional approach to GEOINT as an intelligence discipline and foundation for all operations. Optimization of GEOINT operations is facilitated by unified geospatial intelligence operations (UGO), which is the collaborative and coordinated process to assess, align, and execute GEOINT operations across the NSG and its partner organizations. The GEOINT cell supports joint operations with these seven activities which are not necessarily performed sequentially:

(1) **GEOINT Direction, Planning, and Requirements.** The determination of GEOINT requirements and priorities and the associated strategies, capabilities, plans, programs, and guidance necessary to gather, acquire, create, or maintain GEOINT knowledge, data, products, and services necessary to satisfy expressed or anticipated information needs. GEOINT direction, planning, and requirements are conducted continuously to support routine and core missions and intensify during operation planning and in response to disaster or crisis situations. UGO helps to identify and mitigate unwanted duplication of effort and can facilitate federated support and burden sharing in joint operations.

(2) **GEOINT Discovery and Retrieval.** The procedures and tasks used to search for, find, access, and gather GEOINT information and data from existing holdings, databases, and libraries.

(3) **GEOINT Tasking and Collection.** The collection, acquisition, or procurement of all types of GEOINT sources and the associated tasking and management of collection resources for GEOINT requirements.

(4) **GEOINT Processing and Exploitation.** The assessment, correlation, and conversion of collected data into usable forms or formats suitable for analysis, production, and application by end users. GEOINT processing may include automated, semi-automated, and manual procedures to integrate or conflate data to meet standardized or specified standards.

(5) **GEOINT Analysis, Production, and Visualization.** This information may include finished or unfinished intelligence; standard or tailored products; data; visual presentations of SA; and trend analysis or dynamic operational activities in response to expressed or anticipated requirements and information needs.

(6) **GEOINT Value-Added**

(a) GEOINT data, information, or knowledge resulting from operations performed on existing content that increase its value for subsequent use.

(b) GEOINT value-added may include, but is not limited to, data verification, correction, update, densification, supplementation with additional categories of GEOINT content, reformatting, fusing, or resampling (e.g., color depth, image resolution, date, and location of image).

(7) **GEOINT Dissemination, Sharing, and Storage.** The conveyance, retention, and use of GEOINT data, products, and knowledge in suitable forms and contexts for the individual and collaborative application by end-users and/or partners to support their missions, operations, and tasks.

c. The use of GEOINT can be categorized into four general areas:

(1) **General Military Intelligence and Indications and Warning (I&W).** As one component of general military intelligence and I&W, GEOINT supports monitoring scientific and technological developments and capabilities of foreign military forces for long-term planning purposes and for detecting and reporting foreign developments that could involve a threat to US and partner nations' military, diplomatic, or economic interests or to US citizens abroad. Additionally, GEOINT supports SA by providing I&W of possible increased threats or significant increased tactical positioning of enemy wartime assets.

(2) **Safety of Navigation.** Using bathymetric, hydrographic, maritime safety, gravimetric, aeronautical, atmospheric, and topographic information for sea, air, and land

navigation. The Global Positioning System (GPS) is the primary source of positioning, navigation, and timing information.

(3) **Operational Environment Awareness.** Visualizing the operational environment, tracking movements of interest, and monitoring land installations, support facilities, airfield, and port activity.

(4) **Mission Planning, Rehearsal, and Command and Control (C2).** Employing GEOINT content to plan, rehearse and execute missions, evaluate mission progress, adjust schedules, and assign and apportion forces as appropriate.

Intentionally Blank

CHAPTER II
ROLES AND RESPONSIBILITIES

"Nothing should be neglected to acquire a knowledge of the geography and the military statistics of other states, so as to know their material and moral capacity for attack and defense, as well as the strategic advantages of the two parties."

Renowned Military Strategist, General Antoine Henri de Jomini
Translated from Precis de l'Art de la Guerre, **1838**

1. National and Department of Defense-Level Entities

a. **National System for Geospatial Intelligence.** The NSG is the combination of technology, policies, capabilities, doctrine, activities, people, data, and organizations necessary to produce GEOINT in an integrated, multi-intelligence environment. Operating within the laws of the US, policies and guidelines established by the Director of National Intelligence (DNI), the NSG community consists of members of the IC, Services, Joint Staff, combatant commands (CCMDs), Civil Applications Committee members, international partners, industry, academia, and defense and civil community service providers. The Director of National Geospatial-Intelligence Agency serves as the Department of Defense (DOD) GEOINT manager and the functional manager for the IC, which includes the processes for tasking imagery and geospatial information collection, processing raw data, exploiting geospatial information and IMINT, and analyzing and disseminating information and GEOINT to consumers. The NGA is chartered to do the following: set standards for end-to-end architecture related to GEOINT; produce geospatial information products; provide career and training programs for GEOINT analysts; and supply technical guidance for systems using GEOINT. The Director, NGA has delegated operational responsibility and management for functional GEOINT areas (e.g., analysis and production, source collection management) to senior NGA leadership and knowledgeable staff managing the same or similar activities for NGA. This allows these individuals and their organizational resources to better manage and lead the NSG community and develop related planning, policies, and guidance.

b. **National Geospatial-Intelligence Agency.** By law, NGA is a combat support agency (CSA) as well as a national intelligence organization, and is directly subordinate to the Secretary of Defense (SecDef) and the Under Secretary of Defense for Intelligence (USD[I]). NGA is the primary source for GEOINT analysis, products, data and services at the national level. In addition to the GEOINT support identified in Joint Publication (JP) 2-01, *Joint and National Intelligence Support to Military Operations*, NGA's mission supports national and homeland security, defense policy and force structure, advanced weapons and systems development, and natural disaster relief. NGA is the primary provider of positioning and navigation services to DOD and the IC. Since NGA disseminates data and standard products and makes them available in repositories, GEOINT-trained personnel throughout much of the IC, including military personnel in the field, can access the data to develop their own GEOINT analysis and nonstandard products. Additional NGA roles and responsibilities include:

(1) NGA serves as the DOD lead for all acquisition or exchange of commercial and foreign government-owned imagery-related remote sensing data for DOD components. The agency coordinates such purchases by other United States Government (USG) departments and agencies, on request. This effort facilitates NGA's support to and collaborative efforts with partner nations, other IC agencies, DOD organizations, and other civilian entities. NGA also provides GEOINT strategic workforce planning and specific training for general and specialized tradecraft skills through the National Geospatial-Intelligence College.

(2) NGA provides an National Geospatial-Intelligence Agency support team (NST) in direct support of each CCMD's joint intelligence operations center (JIOC) and maintains an NST at the Joint Staff, Service headquarters (HQ), DOD agencies, and several non-DOD agencies. Each NST is composed of a core cadre that includes geospatial analysts (GAs), imagery analysts (IAs), and staff officers. An NST has reachback connectivity with NGA. The NST coordinates NGA's support to its customers. The NST cadre includes personnel who are trained and ready to deploy with the CCMD's staff at any time. Emergency-essential designation (EED) personnel deploy at the discretion of the host commander and in coordination with the NST chief. The NST chief also represents the GEOINT functional manager and serves ex officio as the UGO manager for the host site. The EED personnel provide deployed on-site GEOINT support in the form of a geospatial support team (GST) to work directly with and augment their military counterparts, and serve as a conduit to the NGA and the remaining NST contingent. At the request of the NST, NGA can provide specific capabilities and additional personnel to the GST structure to meet CCMD mission requirements. The NST HQ element can then provide reachback to the national-level as needed, potentially augmenting any NGA presence as part of a national intelligence support team (NIST), if present.

(3) **Joint Collaboration Cell (JCC).** Co-led by the NGA's Director/Source Operations Group and National Reconnaissance Office's (NRO's) Commander, Aerospace Data Facility-East, the JCC provides time-sensitive GEOINT support to national, strategic, and tactical customers by drawing upon of NGA and NRO processes, capabilities, and subject matter experts.

c. **National Reconnaissance Office.** The NRO is a DOD agency and an element of the IC. NRO is responsible for research and development, acquisition, launch, deployment, and operation of overhead systems and related data processing facilities to collect intelligence and information to support national and departmental missions and other USG needs. The NRO designs, builds, and operates the nation's reconnaissance satellites, which comprise one of the primary collection sources for GEOINT data. The satellites also provide significant imagery to support DOD targeting and mapping requirements and targeting data. Applications of this data include I&W, monitoring of arms control agreements, and the planning and execution of military operations. Once GEOINT data is collected, processed, and stored, NGA takes the lead with analysis and access/distribution for both national and DOD customers. NRO field representatives are located within each of the CCMDs and serve as a direct link to the NRO for the combatant commanders (CCDRs) and their staffs. NRO field representatives provide support covering pre-deployment training, education, weapon system integration, and dissemination of products and services.

d. **National Security Agency (NSA).** The NSA is a CSA and a national intelligence organization subordinate to SecDef and the USD(I). Both NSA's information assurance and foreign signals intelligence (SIGINT) information missions incorporate GEOINT in the agency's day-to-day operations. SIGINT complements and enhances geospatial analysis and becomes an important partner with GEOINT and the NSG. With the implementation of expanding technology and increasing IC collaboration and partnerships, NSA is able to gain a deeper understanding of SIGINT through geospatial associations and pattern analysis.

e. **Central Intelligence Agency (CIA).** CIA is a national-level intelligence agency reporting to the President through the DNI. It provides foreign intelligence on national security topics and conducts counterintelligence activities, special activities, and other functions, as directed by the President. CIA and NGA have liaisons and analysts embedded in each other's agencies. This collaboration ensures integration of GEOINT and other specialized intelligence into the agency's respective functions, products, and missions, providing more robust intelligence capabilities.

f. **Defense Intelligence Agency (DIA).** DIA is a defense intelligence agency designated as a CSA of DOD. It is also designated as a CSA. DIA is responsible for coordinating requirements between the national-level organizations and theater users for the collection of both national and airborne GEOINT.

g. **Defense Logistics Agency (DLA).** DLA is a CSA that provides worldwide logistics support for Military Departments and the CCMDs as well as other DOD components and federal agencies. The director of DLA serves as the DOD integrated material manager for all standard geospatial information and services (GI&S) products.

(1) DLA Mapping Customer Operations (MCO) Division is the supply chain manager for all standard GI&S products in federal supply classes 7641, 7642, 7643, and 7644. MCO is the customer trainer for managing map accounts, ordering maps, and receiving status of orders.

(2) Defense Logistics Agency Distribution Mapping (DDM) operates the wholesale depot and nine retail map support offices (MSOs) located around the world (see Figure II-1). DDM is responsible for storage and distribution of standard GI&S products. The MSOs also provide standard GI&S products and training.

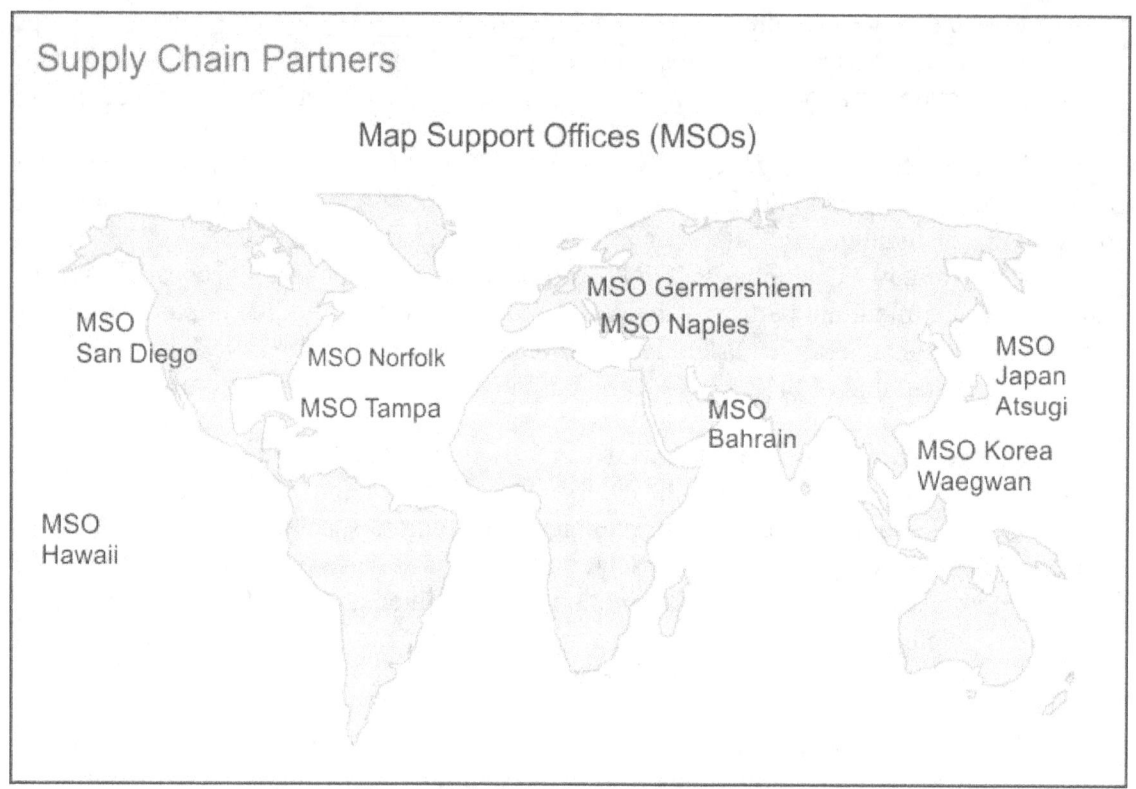

Figure II-1. Supply Chain Partners

(3) Defense Logistic Agency Logistics Information Service produces the DLA Map Catalog. The catalog contains standard GI&S products available in the DLA inventory and is available via digital video disc (DVD) and on-line. The customer information website is at www.aviation.dla.mil/rmf.

2. Joint Staff

The Joint Staff Intelligence Directorate of a Joint staff (J-2) is responsible for GEOINT policy and procedures. The Joint Staff J-2 GEOINT officer interacts with NGA, the Services, and CCMDs to help articulate, refine, and prioritize GEOINT requirements.

3. Combatant Commands

a. The CCMDs develop GEOINT area and point target requirements to support I&W as well as the planning and execution of joint operations. The CCMDs GEOINT cell is responsible for coordinating all GEOINT requirements within its area of responsibility (AOR) while ensuring that the supporting commands or component commands are managing theater and mission-specific GEOINT requirements, to include planning provisions for war reserve.

(1) Each CCMD has also established a JIOC to plan, prepare, integrate, direct, synchronize, and manage continuous, full-spectrum defense intelligence operations. The goal of a JIOC is to integrate all DOD intelligence functions and disciplines, and facilitate

access to all sources of intelligence in a prescribed timeline and appropriate format to positively affect CCMD missions and operations. These organizations facilitate access to all available intelligence sources and analyze, produce, and disseminate accurate and timely all-source intelligence and GEOINT to support planning and execution of military operations. The CCMDs have GI&S and imagery exploitation and analysis capabilities.

(2) The types of GEOINT products generated by the CCMDs include text reports, database entries, target materials and support products, visualization products, and annotated graphics. The GEOINT cell provides advice to the CCDR on all GEOINT information and geodetic sciences. While the CCMDs rely heavily on basic maps, charts, precise coordinates (digital point positioning database [DPPDB]), and other standard geospatial information provided by NGA, they also research, develop, and produce mission-specific, specialized geospatial products and services for the CCDR and components.

b. **Geographic Combatant Commander (GCC) Responsibilities.** GCCs, in conjunction with NGA, are responsible for ensuring the architecture is in place to support theater and mission-specific GEOINT digital logistics.

(1) GCCs have a varying level of organic GEOINT production capability using both NGA- and DIA-provided systems and applications. Production personnel provide tactical and operational data of special interest for use by the NSG, GCCs, multinational partners, and operators.

(2) **War Reserve Stock (WRS).** WRS, a responsibility of GCCs, is one of the three categories of inventory authorized to support SecDef sustainability planning guidance. JP 4-09, *Distribution Operations*, contains in-depth explanations regarding the identification and stocking of war reserve to support CCDR operations, and Title 10, USC, identifies Service responsibilities for identifying war-reserve requirements. The CCMD GEOINT cells should work closely with Service GI&S personnel to ensure that war reserve requirements are properly reviewed, updated, and maintained in peacetime to support crisis or wartime operations.

c. **Functional Combatant Commands**. There are three functional CCMD: United States Strategic Command (USSTRATCOM), United States Transportation Command (USTRANSCOM), and United States Special Operations Command (USSOCOM). They have transregional functional responsibilities that are not bounded by geography.

(1) **USSTRATCOM** has primary responsibility among the CCMDs for US strategic nuclear forces to support the national objective of strategic deterrence and, unless otherwise directed, serves as the single point of contact (POC) for military space operational matters. USSTRATCOM serves as the lead for integrating and synchronizing DOD efforts to combat weapons of mass destruction and is also responsible for providing integrated global strike planning, coordinating transregional information operations, providing warning of missile attacks and planning, integrating, and coordinating global missile defense operations and support for missile defense. USSTRATCOM plans, integrates, and coordinates intelligence, surveillance, and reconnaissance (ISR) in support of strategic and global operations via the Joint Functional Component Command (JFCC) for ISR, as

directed. This USSTRATCOM element formulates recommendations to integrate global ISR capabilities associated with the missions and requirements of DOD ISR assets into the Joint Staff with Commander, USSTRATCOM. As the joint functional manager for ISR, JFCC ISR formulates recommendations to integrate global ISR capabilities and the associated processing, exploitation, and dissemination for the missions and requirements of DOD ISR assets in coordination with Commander, USSTRATCOM, and the geographic CCMDs. Also, under USSTRATCOM, the subunified US Cyber Command centralizes command of cyberspace operations, organizes existing cyberspace resources, and synchronizes defense of US military networks.

(2) **USTRANSCOM** is responsible for providing common user and commercial air, land, and sea transportation, terminal management, and aerial refueling to support the global deployment, employment, sustainment, and redeployment of US forces. USTRANSCOM is also the distribution process owner and global distribution synchronizer. USTRANSCOM's three component commands, Air Mobility Command, Military Sealift Command, and Surface Deployment and Distribution Command, provide intermodal transportation. USTRANSCOM's subordinate command, Joint Enabling Capabilities Command, facilitates rapid establishment of joint force HQ.

(3) **USSOCOM** is responsible for synchronizing planning for global operations against terrorist networks, and will do so in coordination with other CCMDs, the Services, and, as directed, appropriate USG departments and agencies. It is the special operations forces (SOF) joint force provider, and is responsible for SOF training and for integrating and coordinating DOD military information support operations. USSOCOM personnel provide tactical data of special interest for use by the NSG, local commanders, and operators.

4. Subordinate Joint Force Commander

a. Like the CCDRs, subordinate joint force commanders (JFCs) develop area and point target GEOINT requirements to support the planning and execution of joint operations. Accordingly, timely GEOINT support is critical for providing a common framework for visualizing the operational environment.

b. The designation of the GEOINT officer and subsequent establishment of the GEOINT cell is normally done under the direction of the J-2. If there is insufficient expertise or personnel within the J-2 to designate a GEOINT officer or form a GEOINT cell, the J-2 should coordinate additional support from other directorates, NGA, other CCMDs, the Services, or other agencies. NGA personnel, as part of an NST or NIST, may provide reachback support to the GEOINT cell.

c. The GEOINT cell should be fully aware of requirements management for organic and nonorganic allocation and deconfliction in order to assist subordinate JFC's planners in the development of mission-type orders. Effective integration of organic assets with national capabilities minimizes overlap of asset allocation while providing the best data population to local and national databases. The GEOINT cell should identify and resolve communications shortfalls to facilitate GEOINT support. The GEOINT cell should lead the development, coordination, and execution of strategies for the timely collection, production, dissemination, and management of GEOINT data into, within, and out of theater.

5. Services

The Services support their departmental planning functions and CCMDs with GEOINT products, Service-specific content, format, and media. Capabilities exist primarily within the intelligence and geospatial engineering elements. The Services are responsible for ensuring forces train with the appropriate range of GEOINT, and for identifying specific or unique GEOINT requirements for weapons systems. Services also have the responsibility to keep CCMDs informed on Service GEOINT programs and capabilities. Designated Service GI&S functional managers are responsible for coordinating with the CCMD's JIOC and NGA to establish policy regarding roles and responsibilities for co-production, value adding, and management of distributed geospatial libraries. Services will ensure that all systems provided are compatible with the NSG.

a. **United States Army (USA).** GEOINT in the USA supports all aspects of military planning and ground force operations. GEOINT provides a basic framework and is foundational for visualizing and understanding the operational environment, maintaining SA, and making decisions. The Army uses GEOINT by analyzing aeronautical, topographic, hydrographic, littoral, cultural, imagery-based, and atmospheric data that is essential for successful ground combat.

(1) GEOINT support is deeply embedded in field commands. Army GEOINT consists of both GI&S and imagery/IMINIT. The GI&S capabilities of Army GEOINT is provided by geospatial engineering teams at the brigade, division, corps, Special Forces group, and Army Service component command level. These teams provide in-depth geospatial analysis and topographic support, and use distributed common ground system-Army to manage and provide a single sharable geospatial foundation for warfighters, planners, intelligence personnel, and logisticians. Army intelligence units use imagery and terrain feature data from NGA, supplemented by commercial and field-derived information, to produce IMINT and conduct all-source intelligence analysis. Much of the Army GEOINT production and dissemination is conducted on the Army's geospatial intelligence enterprise tasking, processing, exploitation, and dissemination (TPED) service (GETS) web-based system. Army engineer and intelligence units have the latest technology and work closely with the commands at all levels to conduct joint intelligence preparation of the operational environment (JIPOE), produce specialized, tailored views and products, and then support mission execution.

(2) An Army Service component commander may have a geospatial planning cell (GPC) assigned to their command. The GPC is responsible for providing geospatial engineering support; managing, vetting, and value adding new geospatial data to the Theater Geospatial Database, and providing updated data to NGA and subordinate elements via a push or pull process.

b. **United States Marine Corps (USMC).** The USMC uses GEOINT to analyze the topographic impact and climatic conditions on friendly and enemy force capabilities. All related USMC GEOINT efforts support the Marine air-ground task force (MAGTF) in performing its missions. A common geographic reference is critical in supporting any MAGTF operation. Accurate positioning information is key in supporting all of the following warfighting functions: C2, intelligence, fires, protection, movement and maneuver, and sustainment. During rapid response planning, GEOINT provides the initial framework to support visualizing the operational environment. This assists warfighters in developing their courses of action (COAs) as well as conceptualizing possible enemy COAs. The USMC also creates GEOINT products and conducts GEOINT analysis at the Marine Corps Intelligence Activity (MCIA) and out at the fleet which are available to the entire NSG community.

c. **United States Navy.** GEOINT supports the planning and execution of traditional Navy operations such as forward presence, crisis response, deterrence, sea control, and power projection, as well as the nontraditional missions of counterinsurgency, maritime security operations, missile defense, and security cooperation. GEOINT provides the framework for visualization and knowledge of the operational environment. Intelligence units use imagery and feature data from multiple sources, including NGA, to produce imagery, intelligence, and conduct all-source intelligence analysis. The Navy maximizes GEOINT by fusing aeronautical, topographic, hydrographic, littoral, cultural, and geospatially enabled atmospheric and oceanographic data for successful combat rehearsals and operations. The US Navy Oceanographic Office is tasked to collect oceanographic, bathymetric, and hydrographic data in support of Navy and CCMD requirements.

d. **United States Air Force (USAF).** GEOINT is a key component of the integrated ISR capability the USAF provides to (and from) the entire range of air, space, and cyberspace operations. The Air Force distributed common ground/surface system (DCGS) is a principal source for GEOINT derived from theater airborne collection systems, but it takes advantage of national and commercial sources as well, to answer warfighter needs. The National Air and Space Intelligence Center (NASIC), as part of its mission to provide all-source intelligence on air and space systems and technologies for warfighters, acquisition managers, and policy makers, is a leader in full-spectrum GEOINT production. The Air Force Targeting Center includes in its mission GEOINT production such as controlled image base (CIB) for domestic range missions and the operation of the Geospatial Product Library (GPL). USAF civil engineers conduct the installation of the GI&S program to provide the GEOINT foundation supporting base operations around the world, including at expeditionary airfields. The Air Force Weather Agency (AFWA) forecasts worldwide weather conditions, supporting defense and intelligence operations planning. The Air Force Flight Standards Agency has the lead for defining requirements for safety-of-navigation products, such as flight information publications and Digital Aeronautical Flight Information File, for US military aviators.

e. **United States Coast Guard (USCG).** The USCG, one of the nation's five Armed Services, is also a member of the IC and a component of the Department of Homeland Security (DHS). It is the lead federal agency for law enforcement, incident response, homeland security, and disaster management in the maritime environment. GEOINT supports every USCG mission including defense readiness; ports, waterways, and coastal security; drug interdiction; migrant interdiction; marine safety; search and rescue; living marine resources; marine environmental protection; and other law enforcement functions. In addition to producing and leveraging GEOINT for decision advantage within USCG operations, the Service provides GEOINT data and products to IC partners and law enforcement agencies via its sectors, districts, maritime intelligence fusion centers, and the USCG Intelligence Coordination Center GEOINT Branch.

6. Non-Department of Defense Agencies

While US DOD and IC agencies are key GEOINT producers, civil agencies are playing an increasing role supporting operations, whether they are military or humanitarian in nature. As examples, the Department of Interior's United States Geological Survey (USGS) and elements of the DHS participate with the NSG in providing support to defense and civil operations through the acquisition and analysis of commercial imagery and topographic products.

a. **United States Geological Survey.** The USGS, under the US Department of Interior, provides reliable scientific information to describe and understand the Earth; minimize loss of life and property from natural disasters; manage water, biological, energy, and mineral resources; and enhance and protect quality of life. As the nation's largest water, earth, and biological science and civilian mapping agency, the USGS collects, monitors, analyzes, and provides scientific understanding about natural resource conditions, issues, and problems. The USGS also collects imagery in the domestic environment in support of civilian disaster response and recovery missions. USGS facilitates the sharing of information by providing a centralized unclassified repository (http://earthexplorer.usgs.gov/) for dissemination of imagery and map products from the DOD and homeland security communities. The USGS forms cooperative partnerships with organizations from all levels of government and industry. It chairs the Civil Applications Committee, which is an interagency forum that coordinates and oversees the federal civil use of classified collections.

b. **Department of Homeland Security.** The DHS mission depends upon accurate and timely GEOINT focused across the US. Much of the GEOINT data needed for DHS activities comes from local and state sources. Under certain conditions, however, DHS requests and receives GEOINT support from the national IC, principally NGA and through its relationship with United States Northern Command (USNORTHCOM). DHS reviews intelligence oversight and HQ coordination requirements relating to homeland defense and defense support of civil authorities (DSCA) during the planning process. All requests for imagery or other intelligence support for areas within the US are subject to USG intelligence oversight regulations and DOD 5240.1-R, *Procedures Governing the Activities of DOD Intelligence Components that Affect United States Persons.* DOD intelligence component capabilities, resources, and personnel, as a rule, may not be used for activities other than foreign intelligence or counterintelligence, unless that use is specifically approved by SecDef. Executive Order 12333, *United States Intelligence Activities,* and DOD 5240.1-R, allow for the collection of "overhead reconnaissance not directed at specific US persons," which NGA interprets to be in support of homeland security/defense issues, such as disaster response, national security special events, etc. See JP 3-27, *Homeland Defense;* JP 3-28, *Defense Support of Civil Authorities;* DOD 5240.1-R, and DOD Directive 3025.18, *Defense*

Support of Civil Authorities, for additional context to civil authorities. Within DHS, the Federal Emergency Management Agency (FEMA) and the USCG represent important NSG members. FEMA leads the effort to prepare the nation for all hazards and effectively manage federal response and recovery efforts following any national incident. GEOINT is required to accomplish missions ranging from assisting law-enforcement agencies with security, transporting and distributing food and water, conducting search and rescue operations, providing counseling services, hiring and assigning critical personnel, planning for continuity of DOD operations, and coordinating relief efforts.

c. The National Oceanic and Atmospheric Administration (NOAA) has assets and sensors that collect imagery of US coastlines both for research purposes and in support of response and recovery missions during major domestic events. Also part of NOAA is the National Ocean Survey which is responsible for surveying and charting US territorial waters. This includes most US Navy home bases and both hardcopy and electronic charting.

d. Department of Agriculture's National Agriculture Imagery Program is a collection of aerial imagery over the US. This imagery can be used by the GEOINT community and all levels of government. This imagery provides a key baseline data for change detection and other analyses during domestic disaster events and in DSCA operations.

7. Commonwealth Partners

As functional manager of GEOINT and the NSG, the Director, NGA strives to incorporate to the maximum extent its primary commonwealth partners: Australia, Canada, and the United Kingdom (UK). These countries work closely with the US theater CCMD's JIOC on GEOINT production as part of the UGO. While there will always be diversity in the relationships among countries due to varying strategic goals, the desired end state is a common analysis and production agreement for GEOINT. The objective is to work together to respond quickly to the customer's GEOINT needs with the best technology and information.

a. The Allied System for Geospatial Intelligence (ASG) represents the GEOINT relationship among the "five-eyes" community: Australia, Canada, New Zealand, United Kingdom, and United States. The ASG organizational structure is modeled on the NSG, however, all five nations are equally represented. Due to the size and scope of its GEOINT enterprise, the US provides a permanent chair for each ASG forum, while the co-chair positions rotate among the other four member nations.

b. **The United Kingdom.** The focal point for GEOINT in the UK is the Defense Intelligence Joint Environment (DIJE). The DIJE provides strategic direction, policy, and guidance on four-dimensional environmental information (EI) and imagery management, requirements, and capabilities to the Ministry of Defense (MOD) central staffs, commands, agencies, and related organizations. DIJE integrates output from the four existing principal UK Defense EI providers, the Defence Geographic and Imagery Intelligence Agency, the UK Hydrographic Office, the Meteorological Office, and the Number 1 Aeronautical Information and Documentation Unit. The DIJE acts as a single joint directorate to provide vision and formulate policy for EI and imagery management across UK defense. The DIJE also coordinates MOD relationships with other government departments and other organizations arising from bilateral and international agreements relating to EI, IMINT, and measurement and signature intelligence (MASINT).

c. **Australia.** Australia's lead GEOINT agency is the Defence Imagery and Geospatial Organisation (DIGO). DIGO collaborates with the Australian Hydrographic Service and the Royal Australian Air Force Aeronautical Information Service for the provision of maritime and aeronautical geospatial information respectively. DIGO provides GEOINT support to Australia's defense interests and other national objectives. DIGO is responsible for the collection, processing, analysis, and dissemination of imagery and geospatial products, and for determining the standards for imagery and geospatial information within the Australian Defense Organisation.

d. **Canada.** The responsibility for geospatial imagery, meteorology, and oceanography support to the Canadian forces and the Department of National Defense (DND) rests with the J-2 geomatics and imagery (GI) organization. The focus of J-2 support to DND is on meeting the operational and training requirements of the Canadian forces. The J-2 GI organization is located at the National Defense HQ within the J-2 intelligence branch.

e. **New Zealand.** The lead agency for GEOINT in New Zealand, the Geospatial Intelligence Organisation (GIO), is responsible for strategic direction, policy, and guidance to other government agencies on all GEOINT matters. It is situated within the New Zealand Defense Force. The Government Communications Security Bureau contains a GEOINT section, which operates with GIO, and focuses on fused GEOINT to meet national tactical and strategic needs. Land Information New Zealand provides commercial topographic and hydrographic material to customers.

Intentionally Blank

CHAPTER III
JOINT OPERATIONS CONTEXT FOR GEOSPATIAL INTELLIGENCE

"Everything has a place. The better that you can understand the geospatial relationships of the sea, Earth, conditions of the globe and the things on it, the better you are the master of your own destiny."

Mike McConnell, former Director for National Intelligence
Geospatial Intelligence Forum
Volume 7, Issue 6
December 2009

1. Command Joint Intelligence Operations Center

a. JIOCs are established as interdependent operational intelligence organizations capable of integrating all DOD intelligence functions and disciplines in support of the command mission. The primary responsibility of the JIOC is to satisfy the intelligence requirements of the CCMD and subordinate joint forces. The JIOC is the focal point for the CCMD's intelligence planning, collection management, analysis, and production effort, and is organized to satisfy the CCDR's intelligence requirements. Each CCMD, and the two subunified commands (US Forces Korea, a subunified command under United States Pacific Command [USPACOM] and US Cyber Command, a subunified command under USSTRATCOM), operates a JIOC to focus the application of theater and national intelligence capabilities in support of the commands' mission. NGA provides direct support to each of the CCMD JIOCs.

b. The JIOC establishes working relationships and tactics, techniques, and procedures for exchanging intelligence with all potential intelligence contributors. The GEOINT cell should integrate with the JIOC.

2. Joint Geospatial Intelligence Cell

a. The CCMD GEOINT cell is responsible for coordinating all GEOINT requirements within its AOR while ensuring that the supporting commands or component commands are managing theater and mission-specific GEOINT requirements. The GEOINT officer should utilize the UGO process to the fullest extent that is practical to identify existing community GEOINT capabilities that can support operations and avoid unnecessary duplication or redundancy of effort. The GEOINT cell, led by a GEOINT officer, integrates people, processes, and tools using multiple information sources and collaborative analysis to build a shared knowledge of the environment, the adversary, and friendly forces. The GEOINT cell supports not only intelligence processes like JIPOE but also operational processes like the COP and the joint targeting cycle. The GEOINT cell is a group formed by the JFC to accomplish broad GEOINT oversight functions. The cell is normally comprised of representatives from the joint force staff, all components, and if required, component subordinate units and mission partners.

b. A GEOINT cell is tailored based on mission requirements and may include organic and/or supporting assets. GEOINT cell configuration and composition are dependent on CCMD and joint task force (JTF) missions, joint GEOINT requirements, and mission partner participation and/or responsibilities. A joint GEOINT cell should include organic and supporting assets as well as representatives from all mission partners' functional areas. The GEOINT cell can be physically present, distributed via collaborative technologies, or a combination thereof. Mission partners may include DOD, governmental and nongovernmental agencies, partner nations, academia, industry, and multinational organizations.

c. The GEOINT cell facilitates the use of standardized GEOINT processes, procedures, and organizations across the CCMDs, Services, and agencies to enhance organic capabilities to conduct effective joint operations. Organic and reachback capabilities at the JTF level and below must facilitate multi-directional flow of GEOINT within the NSG, to, from, and across the lowest joint level.

d. The recommended composition of the GEOINT cell contains the core and extended cell representatives. As a minimum, the core GEOINT cell should consist of a GEOINT officer, an IA, a GA, a visualization, systems, and data expert, and a requirements plans and management expert. However, these requirements can be tailored to meet the needs of the JFC (see Figure III-1). These personnel function day to day in the cell and coordinate GEOINT capabilities in support of the military mission. An extended GEOINT cell consists of the core personnel plus membership from across the organization and its mission partners to coordinate information fusion, visualization, analysis, and sharing across the military organization.

(1) **Core GEOINT Cell**

(a) **GEOINT Officer:** The GEOINT officer is responsible to coordinate, task, and implement the fusion, visualization, analysis, and sharing of GEOINT. The GEOINT officer is normally a senior member of the staff that is identified early in the planning process.

(b) **Imagery Analyst:** Manages, supervises, and performs imagery activities and functions of the warfighting organization in support of operations and other activities.

(c) **Geospatial Analyst:** Manages, supervises, and performs geospatial activities and functions of the warfighting organization in support of operations and other activities. Geospatial analysis uses accurate georeferenced data and analytic methods to draw conclusions about intelligence issues, and provide specialized services and geospatial products to customers.

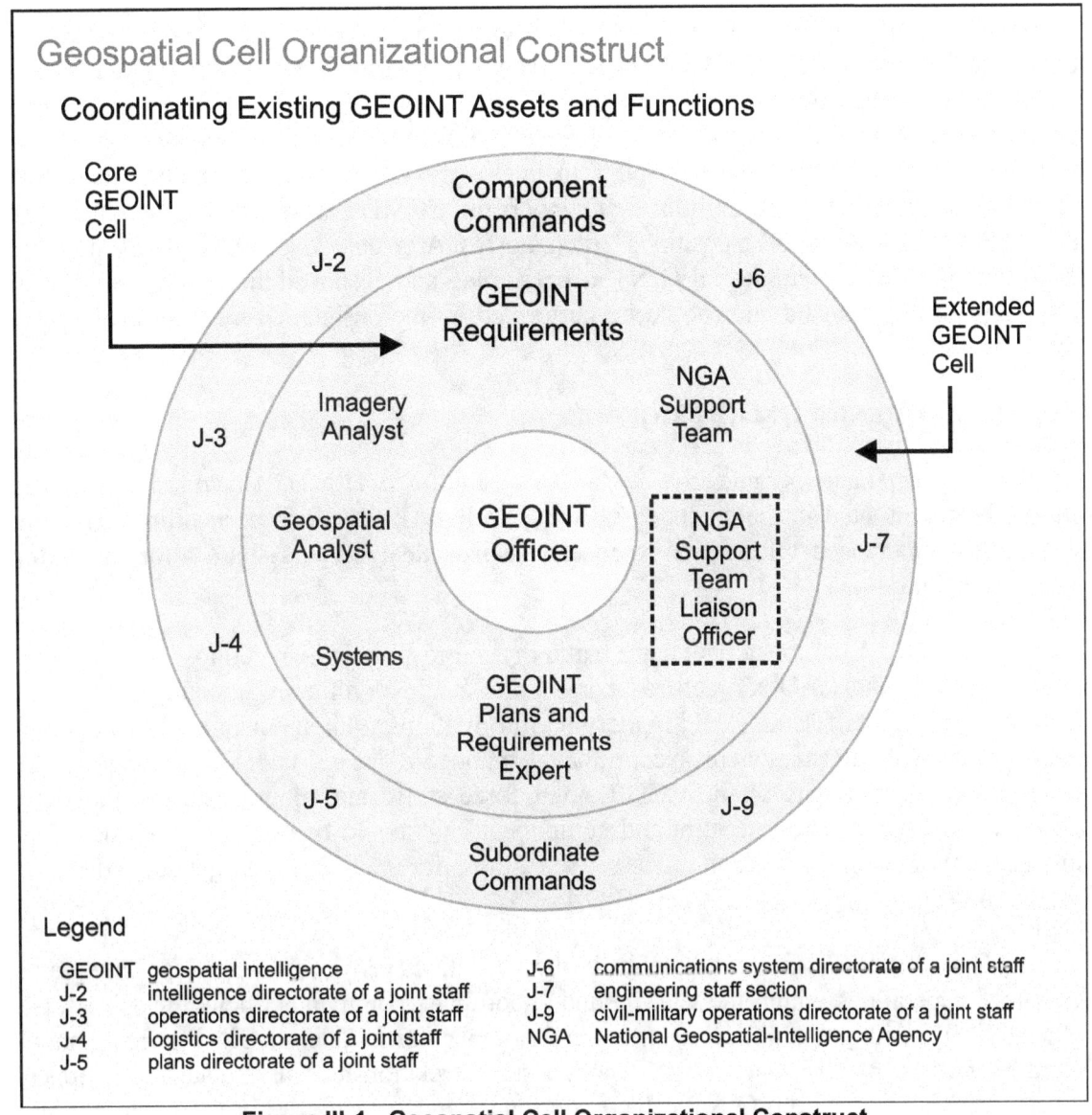

Figure III-1. Geospatial Cell Organizational Construct

(d) **Visualization, Systems, and Data Expert:** Identifies and manages GEOINT data use, storage, and dissemination processes across intelligence, GI&S, and C2 systems. Performs system-level support of multi-user operating systems, hardware and software tools, including installation, configuration, maintenance, and support of these systems (including DCGS, and Global Command and Control Systems). Acts as the GEOINT cell representative to the joint data network operations cell.

(e) **GEOINT Plans and Requirements Expert:** Manages, supervises, and performs GEOINT functional, systems, and area requirements to ensure needs for effective business processes within the military organization are met, including those of mission partners. Depending on the mission, the requirements function may be served by multiple personnel (collections management, request for information management, GI&S production, etc.).

(f) **NGA Support Team:** Advises the CCDR on GEOINT policies, capabilities, doctrine, data, and processes. The NST provides GEOINT capability and expertise in support of the planning and execution of the command's mission and can provide support in the development and assessment of GEOINT requirements for joint weapons and support systems. The NST maintains the GEOINT infrastructure, including libraries and exploitation capabilities that support the CCMDs' mission. An NST member may serve in any of the core positions (often as IA/GA or data visualization, systems, and data experts). However, the GEOINT officer roles and responsibilities are an inherent function of the command and should be performed by the designated member of the joint force.

(2) **Extended GEOINT Cell**

(a) Each organization within the joint force HQ and its mission partners should be represented in the extended GEOINT cell. All functions in a military HQ use geospatially referenced information to fuse, visualize, analyze, and share information for decision making.

(b) A command HQ has a battle rhythm for briefings, meetings, and reporting requirements. The GEOINT cell, as part of the battle rhythm, is essential to support decision making, staff actions, and higher HQ information requirements and to manage the dissemination of information in a coordinated manner. The GEOINT cell supports the information requirements of the CCDR, joint force staff, and subordinate commanders. GEOINT cell meetings of the joint and component HQ should be synchronized and taken into account operating cycles and processes (e.g., those for intelligence, targeting, and the air tasking order).

e. The GEOINT officer will ensure the GEOINT cell coordinates and integrates GEOINT capabilities within the CCMD and subordinate commands, including JTFs, with other CCMDs and national level agencies and organizations. The GEOINT officer should identify and establish mission partner collaborative relationships and reachback support assets necessary for the GEOINT cell to coordinate and manage the broad range of joint GEOINT mission requirements. The GEOINT cell will facilitate communication between the CCMD and the NSG down to the lowest joint level within the command to ensure the timely passing of relevant information.

3. **Joint Intelligence Preparation of the Operational Environment**

a. **JIPOE Overview.** Subordinate commands should utilize compatible GEOINT products, data, and standards to facilitate JIPOE processes and products developed by the joint force J-2 to adequately support the mission. JIPOE is the analytical process used by joint intelligence organizations to produce intelligence assessments, estimates, and other intelligence products in support of the JFC's decision-making process (see Figure III-2).

(1) The JIPOE process is continuous and involves four major steps:

(a) Define the operational environment.

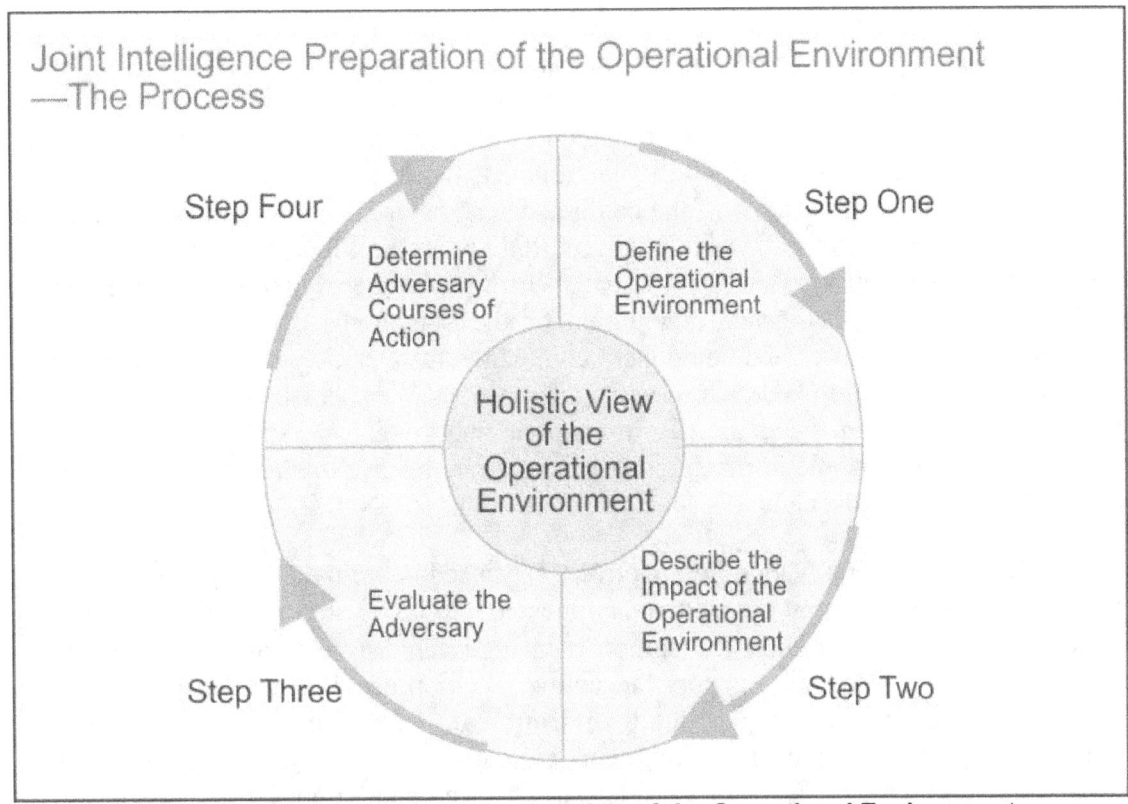

**Figure III-2. Joint Intelligence Preparation of the Operational Environment–
The Process**

(b) Describe the impact of the operational environment.

(c) Evaluate the adversary.

(d) Determine adversary's COA. In this step the staff determines the adversary's most likely COA and the COA presenting the most potential danger to friendly forces and mission accomplishment.

(2) The process is used to analyze the physical domains (air, land, maritime, and space); the information environment (which includes cyberspace); political, military, economic, social, information, and infrastructure systems; and all other relevant aspects of the operational environment to determine an adversary's capabilities to operate within that environment. JIPOE products are used by joint force, component, and supporting command staffs in preparing their estimates and are also applied during the analysis and selection of friendly COAs.

(3) The JIPOE process assists JFCs and their staffs in achieving information superiority by identifying adversary centers of gravity (COGs), focusing intelligence collection at the right time and place, and analyzing the impact of the operational environment on military operations. However, the main focus of JIPOE is on providing predictive all-source intelligence designed to help the JFC discern the adversary's probable intent and most likely future COA.

(4) The J-2s at all levels coordinate and supervise the JIPOE effort to support joint operation planning, enable commanders and other key personnel to visualize the full range of relevant aspects of the operational environment, identify adversary COGs, conduct assessment of friendly and enemy actions, and evaluate potential adversary and friendly COAs. The JIPOE effort must be fully coordinated, synchronized, and integrated with the separate intelligence preparation of the battlespace efforts of the component commands and Service intelligence centers. Additionally, JIPOE relies heavily on inputs from several related, specialized efforts, such as geospatial intelligence preparation of the environment (GPE) and medical intelligence preparation of the operational environment. All staff elements of the joint force and component commands fully participate in the JIPOE effort by providing information and data relative to their areas of expertise. However, JFCs and their subordinate commanders are key in planning and guiding the intelligence effort, and JIPOE plays a critical role in maximizing efficient intelligence operations, determining an acceptable COA, and developing a concept of operations (CONOPS).

b. **Geospatial Intelligence Perspective.** Advanced coordination of GEOINT support is essential among the joint force, national agencies, CCMDs, and multinational and host nation forces in order to form a common point of reference and framework for JIPOE. GEOINT analysts generally support the entire JIPOE process, but specifically **Step 2, describes the impact of the operational environment.** During this step, analysts evaluate the impact of the operational environment on adversary, friendly, and neutral military capabilities and broad COAs. All relevant physical and nonphysical aspects of the operational environment are analyzed to produce a geospatial perspective. A geospatial perspective supports all views of the operational environment by aiding analysis of its physical, nonphysical, and locational aspects. Each aspect of the operational environment is assessed in a two-step process that analyzes its relevant characteristics and evaluates its potential impact on military operations. Additionally, since the physical aspects of the operational environment are not homogeneous, various land and maritime areas may require greater or lesser analysis depending on the relative geographical complexity of the region. Products developed during this step might include, but are not limited to, overlays and matrices that depict the military impact of geography, meteorological and oceanographic (METOC) factors, demographics, and the information environment to include features associated with cyberspace.

c. **JIPOE Coordination Cell.** The JFC may choose to establish a JIPOE coordination cell to assist in integrating and synchronizing the JIPOE effort with supporting organizations, related capabilities, and staff elements. Normally, a J-2 representative will chair the JIPOE coordination cell. Organizations participating in the cell provide advice and assistance regarding the employment of their respective capabilities and activities. The GEOINT officer is normally a member of the JIPOE coordination cell and provides advice and assistance regarding geospatial issues including registering data to a common reference system. The GEOINT officer also assists JIPOE analysts with map backgrounds and data overlays.

d. **Multinational Considerations.** A multinational JIPOE effort requires interoperable GEOINT data, applications, and data exchange capabilities. Information exchange throughout the operational area for the purpose of fostering mutual interests in resolving or deterring conflict or providing support is highly beneficial to all concerned parties; however, it is important to note that disclosure and release of US GEOINT and JIPOE products and information may require foreign disclosure approval.

For more detailed guidance, see JP 2-01.3, Joint Intelligence Preparation of the Operational Environment.

Intentionally Blank

CHAPTER IV
GEOSPATIAL INTELLIGENCE OPERATIONS PROCESS

> *"The commander must thoroughly acquaint himself beforehand with the maps so that he knows dangerous places for chariots and carts, where the water is too deep for wagons; passes in famous mountains, the principal rivers, the locations of highlands and hills; where rushes, forests, and reeds are luxuriant; the road distances; the size of cities and towns; well-known cities and abandoned ones, and where there are flourishing orchards. All this must be known, as well as the way boundaries run in and out."*
>
> **Chinese Poet and Administrator Tu Mu, 803-852,**
> **as found in Wei Liao Tzu (one of ancient China's seven military classics)**

1. Introduction

GEOINT operations are the tasks, activities, and events to collect, manage, analyze, generate, visualize, and provide imagery, IMINT, and geospatial information necessary to support national and defense missions and international arrangements. The GEOINT operations process is described by a set of interrelated and specific activities and procedures that provide SA and support operations (see Figure IV-1). These activities and subtasks, described below, are continuous and may be performed independently, in conjunction with one another, or as a component of other intelligence or operational procedures that require information fusion, visualization, analysis, and sharing. The GEOINT operations process builds upon the intelligence process; TPED capabilities; and joint warfighter interoperable GEOINT process models. It integrates key tasks from each of these into a unified cross-functional approach for GEOINT as an intelligence discipline and foundation for all operational awareness. The GEOINT cell and GEOINT analysts perform each of these seven activities, although not necessarily sequentially or always in conjunction with each other for requirements in support of joint operations.

Geospatial Intelligence Operations Process Activities

- Direction, planning, and requirements management
- Discover and obtain geospatial intelligence
- Task and collection
- Processing and exploitation
- Analysis, production, and visualization
- Value-added
- Dissemination, sharing, and storage

Figure IV-1. Geospatial Intelligence Operations Process Activities

2. Direction, Planning, and Requirements Management

The foremost step in the process is the determination of GEOINT requirements and priorities and the associated strategies, capabilities, plans, programs, and guidance necessary to acquire, create, or maintain GEOINT knowledge, information, data, products, and services. GEOINT direction, planning, and requirements are conducted continuously to support mission information needs during routine operation planning and in response to disaster or crisis situations. The GEOINT direction, planning, and requirements include both GI&S and imagery support.

a. **GEOINT Direction.** The GEOINT cell will develop and publish CCMD GEOINT CONOPS to delineate management of the GEOINT cell and the GEOINT operations process for coordination and collaboration within the CCMD operational processes to maximize the efficiency of GEOINT capabilities. The CCMD GEOINT CONOPS should be consistent with UGO, ongoing GEOINT operations, and NSG and joint guidance.

b. **GEOINT Planning.** The GEOINT cell conducts planning for GEOINT-related needs and operational activities of the CCMD and JTFs. UGO assesses and aligns GEOINT mission, needs, and operational capabilities used to plan and conduct support for routine and crisis operations. GEOINT officers in GEOINT cells work with their organizational UGO officers and manager counterparts to identify and employ GEOINT capabilities across the NSG to support the information and intelligence needs of the command. The GEOINT cell supports the information and intelligence processes for fusion, visualization, analysis, and sharing through the development of supporting plans and requirements for GEOINT.

c. **GEOINT Requirements Management.** The GEOINT cell coordinates across all functions of the command and subordinate commands to identify and prioritize joint GEOINT mission requirements to enable fusion, visualization, analysis, and sharing based upon the assigned mission. GEOINT requirements include the data, information, and product needs for GI&S and imagery to support weapons systems, JTF operations, C2, and intelligence functions. For the purpose of the CCMD GEOINT cell, the process will be generalized as "fusion, visualization, analysis, and sharing" although the order of these activities is not dictated. **Fusion** is the process of examining and integrating all sources of intelligence and information to derive a complete assessment of activity. **Visualization** is the representation of data in a viewable medium or format. Visualization is used to organize spatial data and related information so it can be analyzed and/or displayed as maps, three-dimensional (3-D) scenes, summary charts, tables, time-based views, and schematics. **Analysis** is the conversion of information through integration, evaluation, and interpretation in support of user requirements. **Sharing** is participating in, using, or experiencing jointly or in turns. The following are examples of requirements that are necessary to support mission accomplishment.

(1) The GEOINT cell coordinates joint GEOINT data, information, product, and service requirements to enable fusion, visualization, analysis, and sharing in support of the joint mission. Requirements for GEOINT data, information, and products include, but are not limited to, raw and processed GI&S products, information, and standard and non-standard products. Requirements must include information about area coverage, scale,

timeliness, formats, accuracy, resolution level, updating criteria, data storage, naming conventions, and metadata. Non-standard GI&S and imagery data, information, and products include, but are not limited to, feature data, scanned maps, 3-D scenes, summary charts, tables, time-based views, and schematics.

For further information see Chairman of the Joints Chiefs of Staff Instruction (CJCSI) 3901.01C, Requirements for Geospatial Information and Services.

(2) The GEOINT cell also focuses on joint GEOINT information technology (IT) requirements. It enables the joint warfighter to acquire and operationally employ GEOINT from all sources within the NSG and to provide value-added GEOINT back into the NSG to be discoverable by all. IT requirements include, but are not limited to, systems, standards, hardware, storage, software/applications, and network connectivity of the CCMD, supporting JTFs and components, subordinates, higher HQ, and supporting/supported organizations. The GEOINT cell should coordinate IT capabilities based on available infrastructure and operation/contingency plan.

(3) The GEOINT cell should coordinate with the information assurance manager to ensure requirements are met for database protection, firewalls, public key infrastructure certificates, virtual private networks, intrusion detection, and encryption requirements for GEOINT.

(4) The GEOINT cell recommends releasability, transfer, or disclosure of classified or sensitive information. The GEOINT cell requires the capability to transfer data between network domains.

(5) The CCMD GEOINT cell collaborates with subordinate command GEOINT cells to enable fusion, visualization, analysis, and sharing.

(6) To research existing data/products, the CCMD JIOC or GEOINT cell pulls the needed information from existing sources, or conveys prioritized, validated requests for information (exploitation, production, or analysis) to its designated NGA NST office and UGO manager to deconflict with and prioritize among other CCMDs, the Services, and national agency requirements.

3. Discover and Obtain Geospatial Intelligence

The GEOINT cell coordinates the procedures and manages the tasks to search for, find, access, and gather GEOINT information and data from existing holdings, databases, and libraries. The user can manipulate data from available libraries or databases to create tailored products or data sets for specific mission purposes or military applications (see Appendix G, "Geospatial Intelligence Products and Services"). Available libraries or databases provide the foundation for a DOD-wide distributed network of GEOINT content that includes, but is not limited to topographic, air, space, and other geospatial information, as well as imagery, geographic names, and boundary data. Manual methods and automated services will be used to conduct metadata searches across all security domains to discover existing data and product sources; obtain available GEOINT data and products; identify coverage gaps; and access GEOINT directories, catalogs, web mapping services, and libraries across the NSG. Search parameters should be designed to enable manual and automated discovery of GEOINT based on joint requirements. Parameters include, but are not limited to, classification, content and completeness, resolution, accuracy, projection, datum, coordinate system, currency, and geographic coverage. Once the required GEOINT source or information is obtained, analysts use it to develop knowledge, understand intelligence problems, provide SA, and answer questions.

4. Tasking and Collection

Tasking involves expressing GEOINT needs in the form of collection requirements to appropriate collection assets to acquire data or information necessary to meet mission objectives. Requirements flow through a variety of tasking systems such as GI&S, imagery, intelligence, and other information channels. Collection includes those activities related to the acquisition of GEOINT data or information required to satisfy tasked requirements. Collection activities should be revised as required, and include monitoring the overall satisfaction of these requirements and assessing the effectiveness of the collection strategy to satisfy the original and evolving intelligence and information needs. Collected data or information is distributed via appropriately classified media/circuits to processing and exploitation elements. The process involves converting, via tasking, intelligence or mission requirements into collection requirements, establishing priorities, tasking or coordinating with appropriate collection sources or agencies, monitoring results, and re-tasking, as required. Primary collection systems used by NGA and the DOD community are satellite and airborne platforms and their associated sensors. The GEOINT cell coordinates the collection, acquisition, or procurement of GEOINT sources and the associated tasking and management of collection resources.

a. **Satellite Systems.** Satellite systems are a primary source for classified government and open source commercial imagery collection used to produce GEOINT. These systems utilize multiple sensors to satisfy customer needs. Commercial systems and commercial producers increasingly contribute geospatial information and products for NSG requirements. These systems also can provide unclassified versions of intelligence that, under certain circumstances, may be shared with partner nations.

b. **Airborne Systems**. Government and commercial airborne systems also are primary sources for imagery collection used to produce GEOINT. Airborne systems are managed by the Services and tasked at the theater level and below.

(1) Government airborne systems at the theater and tactical level provide ISR assets operated and managed by the GCC through subordinate components. Airborne systems are neither tasked nor managed by the GEOINT process, although NGA may submit advisory tasking to the appropriate CCMD. The full spectrum of airborne ISR sources includes all manned and unmanned platforms that collect still and full motion imagery using visible, thermal, multiband (multispectral, hyperspectral, and ultraspectral), and laser-based or radar-based imaging sensors.

(2) Commercial airborne systems provide yet another source of GEOINT. Due to their flexibility and resolution capabilities, commercial airborne collectors are increasingly relied upon to augment satellite collection where there is permissive airspace.

c. **Research and Tasking Collection Process**. Taskings requests may be sent up to theater tasking levels or up to national level through a variety of tasking systems. At the national level, the specific tasking systems described below are used to manage requirements for each collection system.

(1) After the GEOINT cell determines that there is a coverage gap or shortfall and new collection is required, it will determine the best type of geospatial collection to satisfy the information need and send the requirement to the CCMD or JTF intelligence collection manager in a format defined by the receiving command.

(2) New imagery tasking requirements for national and commercial systems are prioritized, validated, and passed to the appropriate DIA departmental requirements officer (DRO). The DRO deconflicts and prioritizes with national agencies, the Services, and CCMDs to determine appropriate responses.

(3) New airborne collection requirements are approved by the collection management authority (CMA). The CMA constitutes the authority to establish, prioritize, and validate theater collection requirements, establish sensor tasking guidance, and develop theater collection plans. Although the CMA normally resides at the CCMD, it can be delegated to a subordinate task force as required.

(4) The GEOINT cell will coordinates with the METOC cell to acquire climatology and real-time meteorology, oceanography, and space weather information to support GEOINT collection and dissemination. JP 3-59, *Meteorological and Oceanographic Operations*, contains detailed information on joint METOC operations.

d. **Collection Tasking Mechanisms**

(1) The system used to task national collection systems is the Geospatial Intelligence Information Management Services (GIMS). The GIMS manages intelligence requirements for the national and DOD user community in support of the NSG.

(2) The tasking system used for airborne assets is the Planning Tool for Resource, Integration, Synchronization, and Management (PRISM). PRISM is a web-based application that provides users at the theater level and below with the ability to integrate all intelligence discipline assets with all theater airborne collection requirements. GEOINT personnel have access to PRISM, but actual tasking is a function of the J-2 collection manager.

5. **Processing and Exploitation**

a. The GEOINT cell coordinates the assessment, correlation, and conversion of collected data into a useable form or formats suitable for analysis, production, and application by end users. GEOINT processing may include automated, semi-automated, and manual procedures to integrate or conflate data. After being processed, GEOINT is distributed, archived, and made accessible for users.

b. Exploitation involves the evaluation and manipulation of GEOINT data to extract information related to a list of essential elements of information (EEIs). Exploitation results in the extraction of information and data that is specifically selected for use or integration in subsequent tasks in the GEOINT operations process.

c. There are three phases of imagery exploitation.

(1) Time-dominant exploitation (first-phase exploitation) is the exploitation of newly-acquired imagery within a specified time from receipt of imagery. The purpose of time-dominant exploitation is to satisfy priority requirements of immediate need and/or to identify changes or activity of immediate significance, i.e., I&W. Time-dominant exploitation and reporting is accomplished as soon as possible according to validated intelligence requirements, but not later than 24 hours after receipt of imagery.

(2) Non-time dominant exploitation (second and third phase exploitation)

(a) **Second Phase Exploitation.** The detailed non-time dominant exploitation of imagery scheduled within the bounds of analytic requirements and timelines of need (typically within one week after receipt of imagery). The purpose of second phase exploitation is to provide an organized and comprehensive account of the intelligence derived from validated intelligence requirements tasking.

(b) **Third Phase Exploitation.** In depth, long-range analysis that includes all available sources of imagery and may include information from other sources (SIGINT, human intelligence, MASINT, etc). It is in this phase that detailed, authoritative reports and strategic studies on specified installations, objects, and activities are prepared by the agencies participating in the exploitation effort. Third phase exploitation timelines are not bounded and typically exceed one week after receipt of imagery.

6. Analysis, Production, and Visualization

a. Once data has been processed, it can be used as source to and produce either general intelligence and describe, assess, or visually depict information in standard or tailored GEOINT products. Data can also be combined in a variety of ways to develop tailored products for specific mission requirements. The GEOINT cell coordinates the use, interpretation, and integration of information into intelligence, standard, or tailored products and data, and visual presentations of SA, and trend analysis in response to expressed or anticipated requirements and information needs. During this step of the process, information and intelligence is analyzed, produced and visualized, to satisfy the commander's critical information requirements, priority intelligence requirements, or EEIs. Intelligence and information for joint operations is analyzed, produced, and visualized across all functional areas at each level of command.

b. Through UGO the GEOINT cell facilitates and leverages a collaboration and federated effort in which information is rapidly and fully shared among geographically dispersed organizations. This approach involves assessing, aligning, and executing analysis and production efforts among US and multinational partners to meet the mission requirements of the joint force.

c. GEOINT products include traditional GI&S and imagery products as well as products created by combining geographic and imagery data into a single, multidimensional product. This provides the operational commander with comprehensive, highly detailed, GEOINT products.

d. Once data has been processed, it can be used to produce general intelligence and describe, assess, or visually depict information in standard or tailored GEOINT products. Data can also be combined in a variety of ways to develop tailored products for specific mission requirements, such as evasion charts (EVCs). Producers of the intelligence should coordinate with the users and/or requesters to ensure the products meet mission needs. The main producers include Service exploitation and production centers, NGA, DIA, and the CCMDs' JIOCs. At the CCMD and Service levels, specialized units or sections provide the ability to analyze integrated databases for specific applications, add valuable information or update features and attributes within the database, and strengthen the database content to meet the commander's tailored mission requirements.

e. Categories of GEOINT products and related services and support are listed below.

(1) **Standard GEOINT products** are developed from remotely sensed information and GI&S data. These may be standard products such as imagery readouts, reports, maps (e.g., topographic line maps [TLMs]), charts, and geodetic data, or may be more complex products containing many layers of data ranging from geographic to intelligence information. Standard NGA products, apart from hardcopy, may be rendered in two or three dimensions given the availability of suitable elevation data. In addition, secondary products are often produced for use as references or inclusion into briefs to aid in the decision-making process.

(2) **Specialized products** use standard products as a foundation but provide added capabilities. These products may be developed by using data from multiple sources and multiple intelligence disciplines, and data from advanced sensors. They may also include a fourth dimension—time—providing multi-date context, change detection, and tracking functionality to create dynamic, interactive products. These products can include realistic mission simulations that help determine the impact of currents, tides, wind, daylight, etc., on a mission or intelligence problem and also provide battle damage assessment and indications of enemy activity and improvised explosive devices. Customized products also include products such as: two color multi-view; change detection; interactive maps to visually depict patterns and trends; dynamic images, 3-D models, and a visual picture to provide a common reference and rapid SA for all personnel and organizations involved in the same mission.

(3) **GEOINT services** support the generation, management, and use of GEOINT data and products. These include tools that enable both users and producers to access and manipulate data. Examples are instruction, training, laboratory support, and guidance for

the use of GEOINT data. Types of GEOINT services include on-site technical support, geodetic surveys, software development, tailored geodetic and geophysical products, and validation of software that assesses coordinate derivation for coordinate seeking munitions.

For further information see Appendix G, "Geospatial Intelligence Products and Services," and JP 2-01, Joint and National Intelligence Support to Military Operations.

   f. **Analytic Methodology.** The primary analytic method used to develop GEOINT is called GPE.

   (1) GPE is a process aligned with, and used to support, the military's JIPOE process. A four-step process similar to JIPOE is used, but the information has been modified so that GPE can be understood by both civilian and military personnel and used for both combat and noncombat situations, such as natural disaster relief.

   (2) GPE provides a template to ensure all available data is considered during GEOINT analysis and product development. Although methodical, the process does not inhibit critical thinking. In fact, it requires development of several analytic alternatives. The four steps used for GPE are summarized in Figure IV-2.

7. Value-Added

   GEOINT products are often developed through a collaborative enhancement process based on JIPOE assessments in which both the producer and/or user of GEOINT update or refine a database or product with current, additional, or more detailed information. Enhancing GEOINT consists of operations performed on a foundation of existing GEOINT content that increases its value for subsequent use; value adding may include, but is not limited to, data verification, correction, update, densification, supplementation with additional categories of content, reformatting, fusing, or resampling. New roads, obstacles, and seismic activity, orthorectification, map finishing and 3-D visualization, and intelligence reports are examples of value-added activities that require updating products due to frequent changes. Organic assets (such as special forces, terrain teams, geospatial planning calls or GEOINT cells) take NGA products and add tactical data of special interest for use by local commanders and operators. Value-adding GEOINT improves confidence levels of sources, contributes content, and/or metadata to augment completeness, accuracy or currency of holdings. Ideally, value-adding GEOINT is updated to databases or products that may be readily discovered, retrieved, and used by others. This specialized data shall be centrally stored and catalogued. Intelligence personnel and consumers at all levels must provide timely feedback, throughout the intelligence process, on how well the various intelligence operations perform to meet the commander's requirements.

8. Dissemination, Sharing, and Storage

   a. The GEOINT cell coordinates the conveyance, retention and use of GEOINT data, information, and products in suitable forms and contexts for the individual and collaborative application by end-users and partners to support their missions, operations, and tasks. Dissemination is the timely conveyance of GEOINT content or products in an appropriate form and by any suitable means, whether in hard copy or electronic form, and ensuring that

---

Four Steps of Geospatial Intelligence Preparation of the Environment

The geospatial intelligence (GEOINT) preparation of the environment analytic method is based on, and provides GEOINT support to, the joint intelligence preparation of the operational environment process.

Step 1   **Define the environment:** Gather basic facts needed to outline the exact location of the mission or area of interest. Physical, political, and ethnic boundaries must be determined. The data might include grid coordinates, latitude and longitude, vectors, altitudes, natural boundaries (mountain ranges, rivers, shorelines), etc. This data serves as the foundation for the GEOINT product.

Step 2   **Describe influences of the environment:** Provide descriptive information about the area defined in Step 1. Identify existing natural conditions, infrastructure, and cultural factors. Consider all details that may affect a potential operation in the area: weather, vegetation, roads, facilities, population, languages, social, ethnic, religious, and political factors. Layer this information onto the foundation developed in Step 1.

Step 3   **Assess threats and hazards:** Add intelligence and threat data, drawn from multiple intelligence disciplines, onto the foundation and descriptive information layers (the environment established in the first two steps). This information includes: order of battle; size and strength of enemy or threat; enemy doctrine; the nature, strength, capabilities, and intent of area insurgent groups; and effects of possible weapons of mass destruction threats. Step 3 requires collaboration with national security community counterparts.

Step 4   **Develop analytic conclusions:** Integrate all information from Steps 1-3 to develop analytic conclusions. The emphasis is on developing predictive analysis. In Step 4, the analyst may create models to examine and assess the likely next actions of the threat, the impact of those actions, and the feasibility and impact of countermeasures to threat actions.

Figure IV-2. Four Steps of Geospatial Intelligence Preparation of the Environment

they are discoverable and retrievable by the warfighter on the appropriate network. Dissemination is accomplished through both the "pull" and "push" principles. The pull principle provides intelligence organizations at all levels with direct reachback capability via electronic access to central databases, intelligence files, or other repositories containing GEOINT data and products, as well as to services from other entities. The push principle allows the producers to transmit GEOINT, along with other relevant information, to those who have registered standing interest in certain regions, products, or types of content. Typically, the intelligence staff element at each echelon manages the dissemination of GEOINT. This publication primarily addresses the more common processes used for separate dissemination of GEOINT products.

(1) **Physical Delivery.** DLA distributes geospatial products from NGA to the CCMDs and Services utilizing MCO and DDM. MSOs are established in theater to facilitate GI&S product distribution. The nine current MSOs will be used first, and the determination to create an expeditionary capability will be conducted during the deliberate

or crisis action planning (CAP) processes. NGA may establish in-theater facilities for GEOINT distribution. Commands might also need to establish in-theater distribution points for map depots. Requirements identified in support of the Joint Strategic Capabilities Plan (JSCP) or other contingency planning will be identified and coordinated ahead of time in order to ensure the WRS is maintained at a high level of readiness.

(2) **Electronic Delivery**

(a) NGA provides GEOINT data/products online via the NGA portals and Intelink wiki pages, which are accessible via the Nonsecure Internet Protocol Router Network (NIPRNET), SECRET Internet Protocol Router Network (SIPRNET), and Joint Worldwide Intelligence Communications System (JWICS). It is also available to Australia, Canada, New Zealand and the UK via Stone Ghost and to other international partners via the International Partners Operations Center and national and CCMD electronic transmission systems.

(b) NGA can also support immediate deployment of personnel and equipment to any part of the world at any time through remote geospatial intelligence services (RGS). The RGS team compiles custom GEOINT solutions for military and civilian missions through direct customer interface. RGS has a worldwide presence in direct support of CCMDs and Services. NGA sites in Virginia and Missouri serve as reachback centers. The RGS technical support team maintains the robust RGS equipment including multiple large-format systems for high-volume replication. Software includes a full suite of high-end GI&S tools and image manipulation capability. The RGS analytical team is comprised of employees with a unique combination of backgrounds and skills, including IAs, cartographers, regional analysts, and GAs.

(c) The Services also have developed dissemination capabilities that support standard NGA digital maps and charts (USAF GPL), as well as attributed feature data (USA Theater Geospatial Database). The integration of both of these complementary Service capabilities in a forward theater location provides a robust theater data center that can support the requirements generated at the tactical level.

(d) A system used for the dissemination of intelligence and other intelligence related information is the integrated broadcast service (IBS). IBS disseminates a combined near-real-time combat intelligence picture derived from intelligence sources to operational and intelligence customers at all levels. Another dissemination system is the Global Broadcast Service (GBS). GBS can disseminate large amounts of data in near-real time to a group of users or each user can pull a large file from NGA's web-based access and retrieval portal (WARP) via GBS.

b. There are differences in dissemination methods for data from national, commercial, and airborne systems. The Image Product Library and the USAF GPL provide standard GEOINT and USAF produced GI&S data that might have been derived from all three sources. Separate systems exist as the primary dissemination method for each collection system.

(1) **National.** The National Information Library (NIL) is the primary on-line system for storage of information derived from national imagery systems. The command information library (CIL) and the Direct Feed-Image Product Library are systems that allow higher echelons to make their GEOINT data available to and accessible by lower echelons. Both systems are capable of push and pull dissemination.

(2) **Commercial.** There are several dissemination systems used to distribute information derived from commercial overhead systems. Data for NSG-member use is stored in the St. Louis Information Library, an imagery archive that stores commercial imagery purchased by NGA, in accordance with (IAW) Title 50, USC, and allows users to identify and download commercial imagery. The St. Louis Information Library will be replaced by the unclassified NIL as soon as all existing holdings are transferred. The WARP system electronically receives NGA-purchased imagery from commercial data providers and provides it to users via WARP query and download tools. WARP can also be used to access national source material. WARP is part of the NGA portal and has a presence on JWICS, SIPRNET, and NIPRNET. Appendix G, "Geospatial Intelligence Products and Services," gives a listing of other Service portals and producer sites.

(3) **Airborne.** The DCGS is a family of systems connected through designated points of interoperability designed to provide multi-intelligence discipline, ISR task, post, process, and use capabilities at the JTF level and below through a combination of reachback, forward support, and collaboration. DOD and Service architectures are integrated components of this net-centric joint force intelligence processing and dissemination system. Data collected through DCGS is also available on WARP and can be stored on the NIL and CILs.

Intentionally Blank

APPENDIX A
GEOSPATIAL INTELLIGENCE AND JOINT OPERATION PLANNING

1. Geospatial Intelligence Planning

a. This appendix serves as a guide for GEOINT planning. GEOINT planning activities are aligned with the joint operation planning process steps described in JP 5-0, *Joint Operation Planning* (See Figure A-1).

b. Joint operation planning is an adaptive process occurring in a networked, collaborative environment that requires dialogue among senior leaders, concurrent and parallel plan development, and collaboration across multiple planning levels. Clear strategic guidance and frequent interaction among senior leaders and planners promotes an early, shared understanding of the complex operational problem presented, strategic and military end states, objectives, mission, planning assumptions, considerations, risks, and other key guidance factors. This facilitates responsive plan development and modification, resulting in constantly up-to-date plans. The focus is on developing plans that contain a variety of viable, flexible options for commanders, and in the case of top priority JSCP-tasked plans, for SecDef.

2. Geospatial Intelligence Planning Steps and Activities

a. **Step 1: Planning Initiation.** The detailed discussion of planning initiation is covered in JP 5-0, *Joint Operation Planning*. The extent to which GEOINT subject matter experts will participate in this step of the process will be situation dependent.

The Joint Operation Planning Process	
Step 1	Planning Initiation
Step 2	Mission Analysis
Step 3	Course of Action (COA) Development
Step 4	COA Analysis and Wargaming
Step 5	COA Comparison
Step 6	COA Approval
Step 7	Plan or Order Development

Figure A-1. The Joint Operation Planning Process

b. **Step 2: Mission Analysis.** The commander's staff is responsible for analyzing the mission and proposing the restated mission for approval. Mission analysis is critical because it identifies all specified and implied tasks necessary to accomplish the mission.

(1) **GEOINT Cell Responsibilities during Mission Analysis**

(a) In coordination with the plans directorate of a joint staff, review the operational area of interest (AOI) (latitude/longitude coordinates). Determine if datum issues exist; determine the GEOINT data, information, products, and services required.

(b) Identify deficiencies and request NGA assessment of geospatial coverage for the area.

(c) Assist the J-2 in conducting JIPOE by coordinating the interactive geospatially enabled analytical environment, with supporting digital spatial data, imagery, and analytical tactics, techniques, and procedures, which is linked to multi-source information and intelligence databases and near-real-time information and intelligence feeds.

(d) Identify the required GEOINT capabilities to support the JFC's initial mission analysis process.

(e) Determine specified, implied, and essential GEOINT tasks required to support the commander's proposed mission statement.

(2) **GEOINT Cell Role during In-Progress Review (IPR)**

(a) Support GEOINT-enabled analysis that fuses multi-source intelligence to facilitate IPR; including the provision of GEOINT products and services that enable visualization.

(b) Evaluate the GEOINT tasks, required capabilities, assumptions, and mission statement developed in the initial mission analysis based on the revised mission statement from the IPR.

c. **Step 3: COA Development**

(1) The staff develops COAs to provide unique choices to the commander, all oriented on accomplishing the military end state. It also gives components the maximum latitude for initiative.

(2) **GEOINT Cell Responsibilities during COA Development**

(a) Act as the J-2's GEOINT subject matter expert in the COA development, outlining capabilities and issues.

(b) Provide GEOINT-enabled analytical support (expertise, analytical environment), and information, products, and services (e.g., maps, charts, digital data, and IMINT) to support the COA process.

(c) Identify the required GEOINT capabilities to support the CCDR's concept development and construct the priorities and assumptions on their availability and use.

d. **Step 4: COA Analysis and Wargaming**

(1) COA analysis is described in detail in JP 5-0, *Joint Operation Planning.* While time-consuming, the results of the COA analysis should answer two primary questions: **Can the COA accomplish the mission,** and **is the COA supportable?**

(2) **Wargaming** is a primary means to conduct this analysis. The heart of the commander's estimate process is analysis of multiple COAs. A detailed discussion of wargaming is in JP 5-0, *Joint Operation Planning.*

(3) **GEOINT Cell Guidance for Staff Estimates**

(a) Assist the production of or produce the GEOINT estimate to support each COA.

<u>1</u>. Develop GEOINT tasks.

<u>2</u>. Review assigned and/or apportioned GEOINT forces and capabilities to ensure they are adequate to support the mission statement for each COA.

<u>3</u>. Review and evaluate the GEOINT tasks, required capabilities, and assumptions.

<u>4</u>. Develop coordinating instructions.

(b) Ensure critical GEOINT issues, capabilities, and limitations are identified and communicated in each estimate.

e. **Step 5: COA Comparison**

(1) **The COA Comparison Process.** In COA comparison, the commander and staff evaluate all friendly COAs against established evaluation criteria and select the COA which best accomplishes the mission. The number of evaluation criteria will vary, but there should be enough to differentiate COAs. Consequently, COAs are not compared to each other, but rather they are individually evaluated against the criteria that are established by the staff and commander.

(2) **The GEOINT Cell**

(a) Recommend criteria based on the particular circumstances and relevance to the situation.

(b) Review commander's guidance for relevant criteria.

(c) Identify implicit significant factors relating to the operation.

(d) Identify criteria relating to that GEOINT function.

(e) Coordinate the interactive geospatially-enabled analytical environment with supporting digital spatial data, imagery, and analytical tactics, techniques, and procedures, which is linked to multi-source information and intelligence databases and near-real time information and intelligence feeds that support the finished strategic CONOPS.

f. **Step 6: COA Approval**

(1) **GEOINT Cell Role after COA Selection**

(a) Review the selected COA and determine if any GEOINT tasks, required capabilities, and assumptions require modification.

(b) Ensure that subordinate GEOINT assets receive notification of the approved COA and understand their responsibilities as outlined in the selected COA estimate.

(2) **GEOINT Cell Role during IPR**

(a) Coordinate the interactive geospatially-enabled analytical environment with supporting digital spatial data, imagery, and analytical tactics, techniques, and procedures, which is linked to multi-source information and intelligence databases and near-real time information and intelligence feeds.

(b) After the IPR, evaluate the GEOINT tasks, required capabilities, assumptions, and mission statement to determine if modification is required based upon SecDef guidance.

g. **Step 7: Plan or Order Development.** During this step, the supported commander refines the complete plan while supporting and subordinate commanders, Services, and supporting agencies complete their plans for review and approval. In general, the supported commander will, when required, submit the plans for SecDef's approval. All commanders continue to develop and analyze branches and sequels as required. The supported commander and the Joint Staff continue to evaluate the situation for any changes that would trigger plan refinement, adaptation, termination, or execution.

(1) The CCDR will brief SecDef during the plan assessment IPR of any identified requirements to refine, adapt, terminate, or execute a plan.

(a) Develop the GEOINT portion of the plan.

(b) Ensure that required assigned and/or apportioned GEOINT forces and capabilities are identified in the plan.

(c) Review and evaluate the GEOINT tasks, required capabilities, and assumptions and document them in the plan.

(d) Ensure that all data, information, products, and services outlined in the estimate are available at the times and places required.

(e) Coordinate with all mission partners to determine the structure and composition of required GEOINT data, information products, and services. Of critical importance is to ensure that product formats are compatible and usable by all force participants.

(2) **GEOINT Role in Preparing Final Plan**

(a) If not previously tasked, prepare appendix 7 (Imagery Intelligence) of annex B (Intelligence) and annex M (Geospatial Information and Services).

(b) Ensure all commands have the necessary GEOINT assets and expertise to prepare their command's GEOINT portion of their plan.

(c) Coordinate with all GEOINT assets to deconflict products within the command to ensure all plans are complementary.

(d) Identify any special or unique GEOINT capabilities or products required in the plan and ensure that coordination is conducted, at all echelons, to facilitate their implementation.

(e) Identify all GEOINT cell resources/personnel needed to accomplish GEOINT tasks in all functional areas according to the GEOINT CONOPS, commander's intent, and tasks to subordinate elements.

(f) Task Service components and supporting CCMDs to provide time-phased force and deployment data (TPFDD) for GEOINT personnel and basic loads.

(g) Task Service components and supporting CCMDs include war reserve in the TPFDD (if not already stored in-theater).

(h) Develop GEOINT sustainment flow and related TPFDD in coordination with NGA and DLA.

(i) Task Service components and supporting CCMDs to develop automatic distribution (AD) accounts with DLA to support unit basic load and/or planning stock requirements.

(j) Develop AD listing to cover requirements of CCMD and/or JTF HQ.

(k) Assist staff target planning efforts by providing additional GPE (GEOINT-aided analysis subject-matter expertise, analytical environment, and supporting GEOINT) to fulfill specific requirements (e.g., target system analysis, physical/functional target characterization, collateral effects estimation) associated with development and maintenance of targeting annexes to plans and orders, including the provision of GEOINT products and services that enable the visualization of consequences of execution, and coordination with NGA for such exceptional support as may be required.

(l) Ensure Service components and supporting CCDRs have agreements in place to support en route overflight and access of GEOINT assets and support requirements.

(3) The **GEOINT cell role in developing options** is to be prepared to provide GEOINT estimates and capabilities to support plans and options.

(4) **GEOINT Cell Role to Monitor and Assess.** Assess the performance of the GEOINT process in support of the planning process and advise the J-2 on issues requiring attention.

(5) **GEOINT Cell Role during IPR**

(a) Provide available geospatial and intelligence products, such as maps, charts, digital data, and IMINT to support briefing requirements.

(b) After the IPR, evaluate the GEOINT tasks, required capabilities, assumptions, and mission statement to determine if modification is required based upon SecDef guidance.

For further information on GEOINT planning, see Figure A-2.

GEOSPATIAL INTELLIGENCE PLANNING CHECKLIST		
Steps/Actions	Combatant Command and JTF Actions	GEOINT Cell Actions
Step 1. Planning Initiation		
Initiation	CCDR receives strategic guidance	Review tasking document
Step 2. Mission Analysis		
Mission Analysis	Identify critical assumptions on which to base the plan	In coordination with J-5, review operational area of interest. Determine if datum issues exist; determine the GEOINT data, information, products and services required.
	Identify enemy situation and capabilities	Identify deficiencies and request NGA assessment of GEOINT coverage for the area
		Assist the J-2 in conducting JIPOE by coordinating the available hydrography, terrain, and imagery products as required
		Identify the required GEOINT capabilities to support the CCDR's initial mission analysis process
	Develop list of specified, implied, and essential tasks to be accomplished	Determine specified, implied, subsidiary, and essential GEOINT tasks required to support the CCDR's proposed mission statement
	Create proposed mission statement and desired strategic-	Develop the draft GEOINT mission statement

GEOSPATIAL INTELLIGENCE PLANNING CHECKLIST		
Steps/Actions	Combatant Command and JTF Actions	GEOINT Cell Actions
	operational end state	
	Identify major friendly capabilities and conditions needed for mission success	
	Develop key strategic planning factors and assumptions that may change during planning or execution	Determine acceptable readiness level Coordinate w/NGA on production strategy to fill shortfalls
	Ensure associated scenarios for the plan contain contingencies or other options as required. To do so, analyze scenarios initially provided in strategic guidance statements, confirming them or proposing modifications	
IPR	Incorporate results of SecDef IPRs	Provide available GEOINT products to support IPR briefing Evaluate GEOINT tasks, capabilities, assumptions, and mission statement based on revised mission statement from the IPR
Step 3. COA Development		
COA Development	Conduct COA analysis using wargaming, operational modeling, and initial feasibility assessments	Act as the J-2's GEOINT advisor in the assessment process, outlining capabilities and issues Provide available GEOINT data, information, products, and services as required Identify GEOINT capabilities required to support the CCDR's COA analysis and construct the assumptions on their availability/use
	Evaluate COA comparisons developed during analysis	Compare results of COA analysis to provide best COA recommendation and options
	Select COA recommendation	Keep NGA informed on planning developments/decisions
GEOINT Support to Planning	Develop the intelligence plan that supports the selected COA and associated options	Develop GEOINT portions of the intelligence plan Review and evaluate GEOINT tasks, required capabilities, and assumptions and document them in the plan Review the GEOINT architecture; identify critical components and their status, both outside and within the command Evaluate the architecture to ensure that all data, information, products, and services outlined in the estimate are available at the times and

GEOSPATIAL INTELLIGENCE PLANNING CHECKLIST

Steps/Actions	Combatant Command and JTF Actions	GEOINT Cell Actions
		places listed
		Coordinate with all mission partners of the IC to determine the structure and composition of required GEOINT data, information, products, and services
		Ensure product formats are usable by force components
IPR	Incorporate results of SecDef IPRs	Provide available GEOINT data, information, products, and services to support the IPR briefing to SecDef
		After the IPR, evaluate GEOINT tasks, required capabilities, assumptions, and mission statement to determine if modification is required based upon SecDef guidance
Step 4. COA Analysis		
Staff Estimates	Develop estimate as narrative statement, with supporting graphics	Produce or assist in development of GEOINT estimate to support each COA
		Develop GEOINT tasks
		Review assigned and/or apportioned GEOINT forces and capabilities to ensure they are adequate to support the mission statement for each COA
		Review and evaluate GEOINT tasks, required capabilities, host nation agreements, and assumptions
		Ensure critical GEOINT issues, including legal issues, capabilities, and limitations, are identified and communicated in each estimate
		Keep NGA informed of plans
Strategic Concept	Submit strategic concept/ COA recommendation	Prior to submission, review STRATCON to ensure GEOINT capabilities and level of support are correctly defined
		Coordinate available GEOINT products to support finished STRATCON
Step 5. COA Comparison		
Evaluate COAs	Establish criteria-governing factors	Select GEOINT criteria based on circumstances
		Review command's guidance for relevant criteria
	Create matrix for criteria evaluation	Identify GEOINT factors relating to the operation
		Apply GEOINT support to the finished strategic concept of operations
Step 6. COA Approval		
COA Selection	Communicate COA selection to lower echelons	Review the selected COA and determine if any GEOINT tasks, required capabilities, and assumptions require modification
		Ensure that subordinate GEOINT assets receive notification of the approved COA and understand their responsibilities as outlined in the selected COA

GEOSPATIAL INTELLIGENCE PLANNING CHECKLIST		
Steps/Actions	Combatant Command and JTF Actions	GEOINT Cell Actions
		estimate
Step 7. Plan or Order Development		
Resource Planning	Complete employment, force, support, and functional planning	Develop GEOINT tasks
		Develop initial input for appendix 7 to annex B and annex M
		Review assigned and/or apportioned GEOINT forces and capabilities to ensure they are adequate to support the mission statement for each COA
		Review and evaluate the GEOINT tasks, required capabilities, and assumptions
Sourcing	Complete detailed sourcing	Coordinate with all echelons of source to ensure connectivity and interoperability
		Evaluate required products, identify issues, and make recommendations to the J-2 on how to resolve the issues
Feasibility Analysis	Complete feasibility analyses	Provide evaluation and solutions as required for GEOINT issues
Plan Review	Submit plan summary, basic plan, and required annexes for approval	Provide available GEOINT products to support construction of the plan
In-Progress Review	Resolve IPR issues	Provide available GEOINT products to support the IPR briefings to SecDef
		After the IPR, evaluate the GEOINT tasks, required capabilities, assumptions, and mission statement to determine if modification is required based upon SecDef guidance
Prepare Final Plan	Prepare complete plan while subordinate elements complete their plans for review and approval	Prepare appendix 7 to annex B and annex M
		Ensure all commands have the necessary GEOINT assets and expertise to prepare their command's GEOINT portion of their plan
		Coordinate with all GEOINT assets within the command to ensure all plans are complementary
		Identify any special or unique GEOINT capabilities or products required in the plan and ensure that coordination is conducted, at all echelons, to facilitate their implementation
		Identify all GEOINT cell resources/personnel needed to accomplish GEOINT tasks in all functional areas according to the GEOINT concept of operations, commander's intent, and tasks to subordinate elements
		Task Service components and supporting combatant commands to TPFDD for GEOINT basic loads
		Task Service components and supporting

GEOSPATIAL INTELLIGENCE PLANNING CHECKLIST

Steps/Actions	Combatant Command and JTF Actions	GEOINT Cell Actions
		combatant commands to include war reserve in the TPFDD (if not already stored in-theater)
		Develop GEOINT sustainment flow and related TPFDD in coordination with DLA and NGA
		Task Service components and supporting combatant commands to develop AD accounts with DLA to support unit basic load and/or planning stock requirements

Legend

AD	automatic distribution	J-5	plans directorate of a joint staff
CCDR	combatant commander	JIPOE	joint intelligence preparation of the operational environment
COA	course of action	JTF	joint task force
DLA	Defense Logistics Agency	NGA	National Geospatial-Intelligence Agency
GEOINT	geospatial intelligence		
IC	intelligence community	SecDef	Secretary of Defense
IPR	in-progress review	STRATON	strategic concept
J-2	intelligence directorate of a joint staff	TPFDD	time-phased force and deployment data

Figure A-2. Geospatial Intelligence Planning Checklist

3. Crisis Action Planning

CAP has three broad operational activities: SA, planning, and execution. These activities are aligned with JP 5-0, *Joint Operation Planning* (see Figure A-3).

GEOSPATIAL INTELLIGENCE CELL CRISIS ACTION CHECKLIST

Activity	Actions of Combatant Command/JTF Staff	Actions of GEOINT Cell
Situational Awareness	Begin monitoring and reporting on the situation	Provide available planning maps, nautical and aeronautical charts, imagery, and digital data to the staff
	Establish a crisis action team to track the situation	Understand enemy and friendly situations
	Begin the mission analysis process; define the mission	Understand the boundaries of the AOI and provide warning order to components, DLA, and NGA
	Identify available forces	If required, request GEOINT cell staff augmentation from NGA or Service assets
	Identify major constraints	
	Inform the CJCS of any actions or plans being taken (COA development)	Review CCDR guidance
		Assist the staff in COA development
		Determine what forces and weapons systems are being considered for employment
		Assist the J-2 with the JIPOE

GEOSPATIAL INTELLIGENCE CELL CRISIS ACTION CHECKLIST		
Activity	**Actions of Combatant Command/JTF Staff**	**Actions of GEOINT Cell**
		process
		In conjunction with components, determine area requirements for GEOINT cell support
		Coordinate with subordinate command and supporting combatant command GEOINT cell officers
		Develop GEOINT cell facts and assumptions
		Identify any datum issues in the AOI; make a preliminary recommendation to the J-5
Situational Awareness	Continue mission analysis and situation monitoring	Direct all in-theater GEOINT cell activities (units, map depots) to provide an immediate report
	Review existing OPLANs and operation plans in concept format (CONPLANs) for applicability to the situation	Assess the possibility of multinational operations and related GEOINT cell requirements and/or production capabilities
	Evaluate disposition of assigned and available forces.	Begin release and disclosure assessments
		Continue actions begun in Phase I
	Evaluate status of assigned theater transportation assets. Brief commander as necessary on the situation and ongoing planning actions	Review appendix 7 (Imagery Intelligence), annex B, (Intelligence), and annex M, (GI&S) of similar OPLANs and CONPLANs
		Provide guidance (project codes, quantity limits, priority units, and other related areas) to DLA, subordinate and supporting GEOINT cells for product requisitioning
		Evaluate most current status of GEOINT cell units and activities
		Receive NGA's initial assessment of product and data availability and suitability
		Determine geospatial and imagery data shortfalls
		In conjunction with components and NGA, determine priorities for crisis production
Situational Awareness		Consider substitute products or data production such as single color overprints, image maps, native edition maps, and charts
		Request DLA freeze issue of products that cover the AOI, except small quantities for planning

GEOSPATIAL INTELLIGENCE CELL CRISIS ACTION CHECKLIST		
Activity	Actions of Combatant Command/JTF Staff	Actions of GEOINT Cell
Planning	Receive and evaluate CJCS warning order Develop and evaluate tentative COAs Develop TPFDD With US Transportation Command, conduct transportation feasibility analyses Prepare commander's estimate with analysis of all COAs Provide a recommended COA	Determine what organic or other available Service GEOINT cell assets can support crisis production effort Keep GEOINT activities informed Review the CJCS warning order; ensure GEOINT activities have a copy Determine deadline for the submission of the commander's estimate; determine deadline for GEOINT cell estimate Assist the staff in COA development and recommendation Develop a GEOINT cell concept of operations for each COA under consideration Determine need for map depot establishment in theater Determine GEOINT cell forces required for each COA Prepare a GEOINT cell estimate for each COA Provide a copy of the completed commander's estimate to GEOINT activities
Planning	Continue monitoring the situation and evaluating the impacts on the recommended COA Continue transportation planning Await receipt of the planning order or alert order from the CJCS Await SecDef decision on the selection of a COA Make adjustments to COA based on SecDef and/or CJCS guidance Prepare complete OPORD for SecDef's selected COA	Coordinate with DLA and NGA to "push" essential GEOINT cell products to assigned units Begin preparation of appendix 7 to annex B and annex M When (if) JTF GEOINT cell is assigned, coordinate all actions to avoid duplication of effort Discuss CJCS planning order or alert order with GEOINT activities Complete draft appendix 7 of annex B and annex M; coordinate with GEOINT activities for comment Work with DLA, J-3, and J-4 for transportation planning of GEOINT cell products to deploying units and map depot(s) Work with J-6 to determine paths for distribution of digital GEOINT information to units at both home

GEOSPATIAL INTELLIGENCE CELL CRISIS ACTION CHECKLIST		
Activity	**Actions of Combatant Command/JTF Staff**	**Actions of GEOINT Cell**
		station and forward-deployed sites
		Keep subordinate and supporting command GEOINT cells informed
		Monitor status of GEOINT cell products and units
		Assist subordinate and supporting command GEOINT cells to complete appendix 7 of annex B and annex M
Planning		Maintain contact with GEOINT activities on crisis production, distribution of products, and the availability of information in GEOINT data servers
		Adjust GEOINT cell support in accordance with changes to the published OPORD
		Coordinate with GEOINT activities on the anticipated levels of GEOINT cell sustainment
Execution	Receive CJCS execute order	
	Issue execute order to the designated JTF	

Legend

AOI	area of interest	J-4	logistics directorate of a joint staff
CCDR	combatant commander	J-5	plans directorate of a joint staff
CJCS	Chairman of the Joint Chiefs of Staff	J-6	communications system directorate of a joint staff
COA	course of action	JIPOE	joint intelligence preparation of the operational environment
CONPLAN	concept plan	JTF	joint task force
DLA	Defense Logistics Agency	NGA	National Geospatial-Intelligence Agency
GEOINT	geospatial intelligence	OPLAN	operation plan
GI&S	geospatial information and services	OPORD	operation order
IPR	In progress review	SecDef	Secretary of Defense
J-2	intelligence directorate of a joint staff	TPFDD	time-phased force and deployment data
J-3	operations directorate of a joint staff		

Figure A-3. Geospatial Intelligence Cell Crisis Action Checklist

a. **Situational Awareness**

(1) SA development is a dynamic process that evolves simultaneously with policy. Proper SA development demands that staffs be able to provide immediate advice to commanders, based on contingency planning.

(2) During this activity, a principle task of the GEOINT cell is to develop a commander's situation assessment for GEOINT support. The report must provide current and accurate assessments of the preparedness of the command to execute military operations in the joint operations area (JOA) and monitor the AOI from a GEOINT perspective. The GEOINT cell should make this assessment with input from the appropriate NGA support team. The GEOINT cell's assessment must consider the following factors:

(a) The geographic "footprint" of the JOA and the AOI.

(b) The operational requirements for the command based on the mission and the force structure. The planning factors database can be used to determine what geospatial information is needed by specific weapons and C2 systems.

(c) The availability and currency of geospatial information. That is, what products and data currently reside "on the shelf" at depots and servers, to include available assets provided by the components in the AOR and AOI that can be shared easily to reduce redundant movement/updating of large repositories of GEOINT data.

(d) A preliminary recommendation for what GEOINT cell forces should be included in the JTF.

(e) In conjunction with the communications system directorate of a joint staff (J-6), an initial estimate of the communications requirements needed to transmit digital GEOINT data between forward-deployed units, US production centers, and digital data warehouses, and theater-level computer data servers, and to multinational forces.

(f) The use of interim products such as satellite image maps as an initial deliverable, and meteorological data systems instead of more standard and more detailed digital data. What geospatial information can be developed or updated is a function of requirements and time available.

(3) SecDef's and the Joint Chiefs of Staff analyze the situation assessment and determine whether a military option should be prepared. The CCMD GEOINT cell continues to refine the GEOINT cell assessment and now begins to consider the strategic lift requirements for transporting required geospatial data, information, products, and services of the operational area and the AOI.

(4) The crisis assessment ends with a decision by SecDef to return to the pre-crisis state or to have military options developed for consideration and possible use. SecDef decision provides strategic guidance for joint operation planning and may include specific guidance on the COAs to be developed. The responsibilities of the GEOINT cell during phase II are as follows:

(a) Coordinate with mission partners to ensure that they are informed of the President and SecDef decision and the Chairman of the Joint Chiefs of Staff (CJCS) planning guidance directive.

(b) Provide a recommendation and receive CCDR guidance on the datum to be used for the operation.

(c) Coordinate with DLA to place a hold on distribution of any hardcopy products and digital media covering the AOI. This will allow the GEOINT cell officer to prioritize the distribution of the required data and products to the units involved in the immediate operation.

(d) Develop and provide guidance to subordinate and supporting GEOINT cell staffs, supporting organizations, and appropriate forces regarding special procedures to be used when requisitioning products over the AOI. Information about distribution limits and unit priorities must be established early to prevent depletion of stocks.

(e) Coordinate with the logistics directorate of a joint staff (J-4) as early as possible in the planning effort to determine the impact the transportation infrastructure status has on deployment planning for GEOINT data, information, products, and services, and GEOINT production-capable units.

(f) Coordinate with NGA and the Services for GEOINT cell staff augmentation, if required. NGA has crisis response teams specially trained in requirements planning, GEOINT cell production, distribution, and map depot warehousing operations that can be deployed in theater upon request by the CCDR. The command relationship of NST or NIST support to a JFC will be established in a deployment order. Typically, these teams will be supervised by the J-2 and integrated into the intelligence staff to provide the necessary coordination and support the campaign. The US Army Geospatial Center, the Naval Meteorology and Oceanography Command, USAF expeditionary site mapping programs, the MCIA, and other Service assets may also provide assistance to joint forces as part of their Service components assigned to the operation. Information required by these DOD and Service activities includes justification for request, what expertise is needed, where support will be located, and approximately, when the support will need to be in place.

(g) Coordinate with J-6 to determine bandwidth requirements, impacts, and shortfalls to include all levels of networks. This includes determining availability and source integration of GBS or IBS to facilitate movement of large GEOINT data files.

(h) Coordinate the early geospatial information production and collection efforts of national and theater assets. The CCMD GEOINT cell officer must coordinate with all GEOINT cell producers, including subordinate GEOINT cell units, units from multinational forces, Service assets, and NGA, to eliminate duplication of effort.

(i) Identify, in coordination with the joint force staff, GEOINT cell requirements and/or requests from multinational forces. If required, begin coordinating requests for foreign disclosure and/or release with the GEOINT community.

(j) Establish POCs with multinational forces for supply and receipt of GEOINT cell products and data. Identify foreign disclosure and releasability process.

For further details see DOD Directive 5230.11, Disclosure of Classified Military Information to Foreign Governments and International Organizations.

b. **Planning**

(1) At the beginning of the planning activity, a SecDef decision or CJCS planning directive to develop military options is issued. This directive (and required actions) is described in JP 5-0, *Joint Operation Planning.*

(2) The supported commander analyzes each COA and provides recommendations to SecDef and CJCS. This planning activity ends with submission of the commander's estimate, which includes the GEOINT cell estimate.

(a) The GEOINT cell coordinates with NSG for analysis of all COAs, and determines the supportability of each.

(b) The GEOINT cell supports other staff elements with their planning effort by providing geospatial information or guidance.

(3) The CJCS reviews and evaluates the CCDR's estimate and prepares recommendations and advice for SecDef. SecDef selects a COA and directs that execution planning be accomplished.

(4) An alert order implements SecDef decision and contains sufficient detail to allow the JFC to conduct detailed planning. A CJCS planning order could be issued to initiate execution planning before SecDef selects a COA. The focus of the GEOINT cell staff element shifts to the COA selected by SecDef. In addition, the GEOINT cell officer will complete the following tasks:

(a) Review the checklists found in Figure A-2 and Figure A-3.

(b) Ensure that all subordinate joint force GEOINT cell personnel understand the organizational structures, command, and multinational relationships established for the mission. Subordinate forces and supporting command GEOINT cell personnel should be briefed on key C2 relationships affecting their specific responsibilities.

(c) Coordinate with the operations directorate of a joint staff (J-3), J-4, and DLA MCO to ensure adequate lift and priority is provided for the shipment of paper maps and charts as well as electronic media.

(d) In coordination with the J-6, finalize communications support for the subordinate force GEOINT cell element so that adequate communications bandwidth exists to transmit digital geospatial information from the US to deployed units and data management centers. Develop backup procedures for maintaining support to units if primary communications are lost.

(e) Ensure that requests for theater and national augmentation (both personnel and equipment) are formally submitted and responses are tracked. Coordinate with the manpower and personnel officer to ensure that logistic preparations for locating and housing augmentees are underway. As directed, the NSG will provide support teams and analysts to theater joint intelligence/analysis centers to directly support the highest and most urgent intelligence needs.

(f) Coordinate final personnel, systems, supply, and equipment requirements with the subordinate GEOINT cell officer and ensure that these requirements are submitted to the Joint Operation Planning and Execution System and the TPFDD.

(g) Resolve foreign disclosure and/or release policies with respect to GEOINT and inform subordinate GEOINT cell personnel of these procedures IAW US law. Requirements to share geospatial data must be finalized and specific products or data to be shared must be identified in annex M (GI&S), in the operation order (OPORD). Coordinate with NGA for support being provided to multinational forces through the United Nations, North Atlantic Treaty Organization, or other intergovernmental organizations.

(h) Obtain status from NGA on their crisis production plan to cover GEOINT cell shortfalls.

(i) Begin coordination with DLA and Services on in-theater regional map depot and manning requirements.

(j) Seek staff judge advocate review of the status of in-place bilateral and/or multilateral diplomatic agreements to support en route overflight and access of GEOINT assets and personnel.

(5) The approved CJCS COA is transformed into an OPORD. Detailed planning occurs throughout the joint planning community. If required, the supported commander will initiate campaign planning or refine a campaign plan already developed.

(6) The supported commander develops the OPORD and supporting TPFDD by modifying an existing operation plan (OPLAN), expanding an existing concept plan (CONPLAN), or developing a new plan. This phase ends with a SecDef decision to implement the OPORD. In those instances where the crisis does not progress to implementation, the CJCS provides guidance on continued planning using either deliberate planning or CAP procedures.

(a) The planning emphasis shifts to transportation requirements and the building of movement schedules. The movement status of GEOINT cell forces, equipment, and GEOINT data should be included in every status report and briefing prepared during the planning of joint operations. Emphasis should be placed on ensuring required aircraft diplomatic clearance timelines outlined in the DOD *Electronic Foreign Clearance Guide*, are considered. The guide can be accessed at https://www.fcg.pentagon.mil/fcg.cfm, and is also available on SIPRNET at http://www.fcg.pentagon.smil.mil.

(b) GEOINT cell actions include the following:

__1.__ Brief subordinate GEOINT cell officers, DLA, NGA, and Service GEOINT support activities on the alert or planning order.

__2.__ Finalize any remaining planning or previous actions that were compressed due to the rapid development of the crisis.

__3.__ Refine appendix 7 (Imagery Intelligence) to annex B (Intelligence) and annex M (GI&S) to the OPORD according to Chairman of the Joint Chiefs of Staff Manual (CJCSM) 3130.03, *Adaptive Planning and Execution (APEX) Planning Formats and Guidance.* See Appendix C, "Sample Annex M (Geospatial Information and Services)" and appendix 7 (Imagery Intelligence) to annex B (Intelligence).

__4.__ Ensure that all subordinate GEOINT cell personnel understand the GEOINT cell support operations concept.

__5.__ Ensure that C2 relationships have been defined for GEOINT cell support to major component forces of the subordinate joint force.

__6.__ Apprise the commander of the current status of GEOINT cell capabilities and limitations as well as the status of crisis production of GEOINT.

__7.__ Brief personnel on the complete OPORD.

c. **Execution.** Execution begins when the President or SecDef decides to use a military option to resolve a crisis. Only the President or SecDef can authorize the CJCS to issue an execute order (EXORD). The EXORD directs the supported commander to initiate military operations, defines the time to initiate operations, and conveys guidance not provided earlier. The CJCS monitors the deployment and employment of forces, and advises and makes recommendations to the President, the National Security Council, and SecDef on the operation. USTRANSCOM provides common-user and commercial global air, land, and sea transportation, reporting the progress of deployments to the CJCS and the supported commander. Execution continues until the operation is terminated or the mission is accomplished or revised. The CAP process may be repeated continuously as circumstances and missions change. As soon as the deployment begins, the command GEOINT cell coordinates the deployment of requested GEOINT cell augmentation of personnel and/or equipment to the theater. The command GEOINT cell continues to provide production guidance to NSG and suggests GEOINT collection requirements to theater commands until the subordinate joint force GEOINT cell staff has reached operational status at the deployed location.

APPENDIX B
GEOSPATIAL INTELLIGENCE ESTIMATE

The GEOINT estimate is an appraisal of available GEOINT for a specific situation in a certain region of the world. It is used to determine the supportability of a COA, depending upon the GEOINT requirements for planning and execution. The format for the GEOINT estimate is provided as follows:

CLASSIFICATION

Originating Section Issuing Headquarters
Classified documents mandate appropriate marking and
Sourcing--which for derivative classifiers include a
CL BY
DER FROM
DECL ON
or Original classifiers of
CL BY
CL REASON
DECL ON

(Note: When this estimate is distributed outside the issuing HQ, the first line of the heading is the official designation of the issuing command, and the ending of the estimate is modified to include authentication by the authorizing section, division, or other official according to local policy.)

Place of Issue

Day, Month, Year

GEOINT STAFF ESTIMATE NUMBER

(Note: Normally, these are numbered sequentially during a calendar year.)

( ) REFERENCES:

    a. GEOINT data, information, products, and services.

    b. Other relevant documents.

1. ( ) Mission. State the assigned task and its purpose. The mission of the overall command is taken from the commander's mission analysis, planning guidance, or other statement.

2. ( ) Situation

a. Definition of the AOI. Describe the limits of the AOI both in terms of natural or cultural features and latitude and longitude coordinates. If the AOI limits are difficult to describe, a map with the appropriate boundaries should be appended. Appropriate imagery should also be used whenever possible.

b. Assigned or apportioned GEOINT assets. Identify those forces that can perform one or more of the following GEOINT functions:

    (1) Map and chart distribution.

    (2) Direct machine-to-machine access (e.g., Internet protocol addresses).

    (3) Digital dissemination of data and/or information.

    (4) Analysis of the operational environment.

    (5) Paper map or chart production and reproduction.

    (6) Digital data production.

    (7) Geodetic surveying.

    (8) C2 of GEOINT assets.

    (9) Geospatial database management.

    (10) Value-added to GEOINT data sets.

    (11) Construction of modeling and/or simulation databases.

    (12) Geospatial analysis.

    (13) GPS SA.

    (14) Imagery.

    (15) Imagery analysis.

    (16) Access to GEOINT libraries.

c. Facts and assumptions. Facts and assumptions are usually generated during the mission analysis process, and may include items such as release and disclosure of GEOINT products to multinational forces, transportation availability, and digital communications availability and other topics as necessary.

d. GEOINT considerations. Example items are:

(1) Datum determination, horizontal as well as vertical references to height above ellipsoid and or mean sea level.

(2) Availability of standard GEOINT data, information, products, and services.

(3) Currency of data, information, and products.

(4) Availability of imagery from national and commercial sources.

(5) GEOINT support to and from multinational forces.

(6) Existing GEOINT agreements with foreign countries.

(7) WRS and basic load considerations.

(8) Maintenance of GEOINT data.

(9) Sustainment of GEOINT assets and personnel.

(10) Creation and manning of forward map depots.

(11) Data, information, products, and services requirements for mission rehearsal areas.

(12) Local availability of networks and online GEOINT data, products, and services.

(13) Distribution of hardcopy products.

(14) Supplemental manning of MSO.

(15) Disclosure or release to multinational partners.

3. ( ) Analysis of COAs. The following are examples of factors the GEOINT cell can use to weigh COAs:

a. GEOINT forces and functions: The COA employs forces to cover the greatest number of GEOINT functions.

b. Datums and interoperability: Assesses each COA for datum and format transformations needed to support forces within the AOI.

c. Multinational partner operations: Assessment of how each COA facilitates operations and what support is required of other nations.

d. GEOINT coverage: Assessment of each COA for the availability of GEOINT data and information over the AOI (if COAs have somewhat different geographic boundaries).

e. NGA supportability: An assessment by COA from an NGA supportability perspective.

f. Simplicity of GEOINT distribution and digital dissemination: Assessment by COA of the probable scheme for distributing paper maps and charts and the digital dissemination of GEOINT data.

g. C2 of GEOINT assets: Assessment of the COA from a C2 perspective.

h. Unit basic loads and WRS: Assessment of the COA for requirements by operational forces for both paper and digital geospatial data.

4. ( ) Comparison of COAs. Using the factors stated above and others, the GEOINT cell compares the different COAs to determine if GEOINT supportability is a factor for execution.

5. ( ) Conclusions. Once the analysis is complete, the GEOINT cell should either make a recommendation for a single COA, or state that none of the COAs are adversely affected by the current GEOINT situation.

(signed)

_____

(Note: The staff division chief [J-2] signs the GEOINT cell estimate. If the estimate is to be distributed outside the HQ, the heading and signature block must be changed to reflect that fact.)

ANNEXES: (By letter and title) Annexes should be included where the information is in graphs (such as geospatial data coverage graphics) or is of such detail and volume that inclusion makes the body of the estimate cumbersome. They should be lettered sequentially as they occur throughout the estimate.

DISTRIBUTION: (According to procedures and policies of the issuing HQ)

CLASSIFICATION

Copy no.   of   copies

OFFICIAL DESIGNATION OF COMMAND

CL BY

DER FROM

DECL ON

Or Original classifiers of

CL BY

CL REASON

DECL ON

PLACE OF ISSUE

Date/time group

Message reference number

(U) References:

(a) (U) List JTF, other components, theater and national intelligence and counterintelligence plans, orders, tactics, techniques, and procedures, as well as multinational agreements pertinent to the operation.

(b) (U) List those NGA maps, nautical and aeronautical charts, and related products, and other forms of GI&S data references required for an understanding of this annex.

(c) (U) List other relevant documents that provide guidance required for the necessary planning functions relevant to GI&S and supporting operations.

1. (U) SITUATION

a. (U) GI&S Requirements. Operations will require aeronautical, hydrographic, and topographic paper and digital products. Area coverage requirements as well as a detailed listing by NGA Reference Number (NRN) or product/sheet number, National Stock Number (NSN) and edition number are listed in Appendix 1—Geospatial Information and Services Requirements List:

(1) (U) City Graphics.

(2) (U) 1:25,000 Topographic Line Maps.

(3) (U) 1:50,000 Topographic Line Maps.

(4) (U) 1:100,000 Topographic Line Maps.

(5) (U) 1:250,000 Joint Operations Graphics.

(6) (U) 1:500,000 Tactical Pilotage Charts.

(7) (U) 1:1,000,000 Operational Navigation Charts.

(8) (U) 1:2,000,000 Jet Navigation Charts.

(9) (U) 1:5,000,000 Global Navigation and Planning Charts.

(10) (U) Coastal Charts.

(11) (U) Pilot Charts.

(12) (U) Sailing Charts.

(13) (U) 1:50,000 Littoral Planning Charts.

(14) (U) Approach Charts.

(15) (U) Digital Bathymetric Database (DBDB).

(16) (U) Harbor/Approach Charts.

(17) (U) Digital Nautical Chart (DNC).

(18) (U) Geospatial intelligence base for contingency operations (GIBCO).

(19) (U) Digital Terrain Elevation Data (DTED) Levels 1-2.

(20) (U) High resolution elevation (HRE).

(21) (U) Foreign-produced Tourist Maps.

(22) (U) Escape and Evasion Charts.

(23) (U) Controlled Image Base (CIB) 1 and 5 Meter.

(24) (U) Digital Point Positioning Database (DPPDB).

(25) (U) GeoPDF maps.

(26) (U) Shuttle Radar Topography Mission DTED.

(27) (U) Various scales, image city map (ICM).

(28) (U) Image map for each of the TLM scales.

(29) (U) Compressed ARC Digitized Raster Graphic (CADRG).

(30) (U) Precise Orthorectified Image Dataset (POID) and or Commercial Orthorectified Image Product (COIP).

(31) (U) Enhanced Compressed Raster Graphics (ECRG).

(32) (U) Enhanced Controlled Image Base (eCIB).

(33) (U) Tactical Ocean Data (TOD) Level 0.

(34) (U) Tactical Ocean Data (TOD) Level 1.

(35) (U) Tactical Ocean Data (TOD) Level 2.

(36) Tactical Ocean Data (TOD) Level 3.

(37) (U) Tactical Ocean Data (TOD) Level 4.

(38) (U) Global Topographic Data Store (GTDS) vector feature data.

(39) (U) Regional Topographic Data Store (STDS) vector feature data.

(40) (U) Local Topographic Data Store (LTDS) vector feature data.

(41) (U) Specialized/Urban Topographic Data Store (S/UTDS) vector feature data.

b. (U) Enemy. Refer to Annex B (Intelligence) of the OPORD for the basic enemy situation.

c. (U) Friendly Support. Refer to Annex C of the OPORD. List the GI&S forces or agencies that are not assigned or attached to the unit but that will be required to provide GI&S support for the implementation of this order. Specify the type of command relationship desired for each agency or command and the type and duration of support required.

(1) (U) NGA.

(2) (U) NGA Support Team.

(3) (U) DIA.

(4) (U) CCMD's JIOC.

(5) (U) Service geospatial production activities (AGC, NAVO, etc).

(6) (U) Department of State/US.

(7) DLA.

d. (U) Assumptions. List any assumptions on which this annex is based. State expected conditions pertinent to GI&S support over which the commander has no control. Describe planning and early deployment assumptions concerning the availability of basic loads and DLA's and NGA's ability to meet crisis demand.

(1) (U) GI&S requirements represent classified and unclassified aeronautical, hydrographic, topographic, and GEOINT targeting support materials.

(2) (U) The CCDR will coordinate all requirements for out-of-theater support, including aircraft diplomatic clearances and generation of precise points for targeting support.

(3) (U) The CCDR's GI&S officer will appoint the theater geospatial database manager and will publish requirements for reports, generation, information requests, and tasking authority.

(4) (U) Component commanders and planning staffs will have required operational quantities of maps, charts, and digital data to conduct operational-level planning.

(5) (U) Sufficient warning prior to execution will allow NGA to meet increased requirements through crisis support systems.

e. (U) Available Products. Provide a general statement regarding the availability and adequacy of the listed GI&S data, products, and related material required to support the OPORD. For example: complete coverage consisting of topographic, hydrographic, and aeronautical products exists to support this OPORD. In some areas 1:100,000 scale imagery may be used to support operations.

f. (U) Available Services. Describe any special geospatial services that will be provided for the operation, e.g., precise production, data transformations, commercial imagery purchase, and orthorectification and geodetic surveying. Identify those GI&S units assigned or attached in theater. List information concerning other forces or agencies outside theater that may affect the provision of GI&S products. Include a list of available uniform resource locators and internet protocol addresses.

g. (U) Capabilities. List those GI&S forces organic, assigned, or attached to the unit. Show latest arrival date at point of departure for each GI&S unit and list information concerning other forces or agencies that may affect the provisions of GI&S products required to support the OPORD.

2. (U) MISSION. Provide a clear, concise statement of the GI&S mission in support of the OPORD.

3. (U) EXECUTION

    a. (U) Concept of GI&S Operations

        (1) (U) General. Provide a broad statement of how the command will provide the GI&S support necessary to meet the commander's overall mission requirement. Include the organic units and supporting units involved; the time-phasing of operations; the general nature and purpose of GI&S operations to be conducted; the interrelated or cross-Service support; and support provided by agreements, coordination, and cooperation necessary for the successful implementation of the OPORD. Describe the scope and extent of host nation support available to enhance operations in support of the OPORD.

        (a) (U) Forces deploying in support of this OPORD are required to arrive with a 30-day basic load of GI&S products.

        (b) (U) Resupply or sustainment stocks and follow-on supplies of maps and charts will be provided via normal supply channels.

        (c) (U) Substitute products and interim products may be provided by NGA and other Service agencies to supplement available coverage.

        (d) (U) Subordinate units with GI&S assets retain primary responsibility for their own quick-response products.

        (e) (U) Supporting plans will specify the required maps, nautical and aeronautical charts, and digital databases; terrain analysis requirements; cartographic and geodetic survey requirements; procedures for requesting standard and/or nonstandard topographic production support; and guidance for hardcopy and digital distribution. Requirements for special products and materials will also be included in supporting plans.

        (2) (U) Deployment. Summarize the requirements for deploying organic GI&S forces and necessary depot activities from their normal peacetime locations to the operational area. Pay particular attention to the time-phasing of these deployments in order to affect an orderly transition from current to planned organizational configurations.

        (a) (U) Subordinate units will ensure communications connectivity for attached units.

        (b) (U) Subordinate units will maintain and deploy with a 30-day basic load of GI&S stocks.

        (c) (U) Automatic distribution change requests and updates for validation will be forwarded to the JTF.

        (d) (U) All subordinate units will update the list of deployment and GI&S basic load requirements and submit these to the appropriate unit.

(e) (U) Basic load airlift or sealift transportation from the US to the port of entry will be arranged per requirements outlined in the current DOD Foreign Clearance Guide, established time-phased force and deployment list procedures, and established transportation priorities.

(3) (U) Transportation and movement of WRS or sustainment stocks to subordinate units will be coordinated with JTF supply and MSO.

(4) (U) Employment. Describe in general terms how the GI&S forces are to be employed in the conduct of operations. Commanders will employ GI&S units to accomplish tasks assigned. Outside theater units will push GI&S products forward. Standard GI&S products will go to Unit XYZ, which will establish a map depot within the supply support activity (SSA). Special GI&S products will go to the requesting unit. This paragraph must explain how each unit will be employed to execute the GI&S plan. It must also be time phased to fit into the TPFDD and OPLAN.

(5) (U) Interoperability. Provide specific technical guidance and procedures to ensure interoperability of GI&S operations and materials, particularly the proper sources, datum documentation, and use of coordinates derived from GI&S products. Provide guidance to ensure that sources, methods, and procedures result in the required accuracy.

b. (U) Tasks. In separate numbered subparagraphs, list the GI&S tasks assigned to each element of the JTF and to those supporting external units or agencies. For each of the tasks, provide a concise mission statement to be performed in further planning or execution of the JTF OPORD. Provide sufficient details in these task assignments to ensure that essential elements to the concept of operation are described properly.

(1) (U) Commander, XXX Unit.

(a) (U) Act as the POC for all xxx component GI&S issues.

(b) (U) Coordinate all validated GI&S collection, production, and dissemination requirements with the JTF. Forward all requirements to CCMD GEOINT cell for consolidation and submission to NGA or other GEOINT activity for action.

(2) (U) Commander, YYY Unit.

(a) (U) Ensure that sufficient GI&S standard products are available for all units at deployment locations.

(b) (U) Provide resupply of GI&S standard products as requested.

(3) (U) GI&S Unit ZZZ.

(a) (U) Provide a single POC for GI&S planning and support.

(b) (U) Provide GI&S nonstandard product support.

(c) (U) Coordinate with CCMD for GI&S support.

c. (U) Coordinating Instructions. List in separate numbered subparagraphs the instructions applicable to two or more elements of the JTF and supporting units/agencies that are necessary for proper coordination of the GI&S support. Specify the POCs within the command that can authorize the release of WRS held or that can resolve command GI&S problems. Also, include a brief description of how notification of forces and agencies will be accomplished and time sequencing of notifications.

(1) (U) Subordinate units will review the OPLAN for GI&S requirements and identify errors or shortfalls through their chain of command to the JTF GEOINT cell no later than 5 days following receipt of OPLAN.

(2) (U) Ensure basic load, as determined by the unit, of required maps, charts, geodetic data, and related materials accompanying deploying units are identified and stocked at supporting components depots, along with a distribution plan to meet the needs of assigned forces.

(3) (U) Units with print/reproduction capabilities. Be prepared to reproduce limited quantities of existing maps of operational areas if required. Reproduction may include overlaying/overprinting lines of communications, helicopter landing zones, staging/assembly areas, or other information significant to the tactical commander.

(4) (U) Provide transportation to move maps, nautical and aeronautical charts, and related materials with deploying forces. Within theater of operations, map, chart, and geodetic data transfer is a supply point operation.

(5) (U) Positions will be referenced to the World Geodetic System 1984. Ground units and ground combat operations will be serviced with military grid reference system (MGRS). The complete grid will be used to transmit coordinates. In aviation and nautical operations, latitude and longitude positions will be given in degrees/minutes-decimal-minutes format. However, different platforms may require different formats such as degrees, minutes, seconds, or decimal seconds to import data directly into required mission planning/execution equipment. Decimal minutes is the most common but not the only required format.

4. (U) Administration and Logistics

a. (U) Supply and Storage. Provide instructions regarding GI&S supply and storage procedures and responsibilities. Include the planned locations of command and non-command storage sites and facilities. Refer to the command GI&S WRS plan to define detailed packaging and activation instructions at storage facilities. Specify the types and quantities of products or timeframe required to be held by the supporting command's units or agencies. Outline the intratheater distribution plan to be implemented by unit logistic organizations.

b. (U) Transportation. Provide general instructions regarding GI&S material transportation requirements. Use a separate appendix to list detailed transportation requirements and procedures.

(1) (U) DLA will ship maps to authorized customers and its regional MSOs/SSAs. Major subordinate units are responsible for transporting maps and charts to/from depots within the theater. (Transportation responsibilities need to be coordinated with the overall logistics plan, with specific units assigned transportation responsibilities for each depot. Without this coordination, maps will be forgotten in the overall plan.)

(2) (U) The JTF mission drives the number of materials needed for support. For example, the JTF will require approximately 940,000 paper maps, weighing approximately 115,000 lbs., within 60 days after D-Day. Approximately eight standard 463L pallets will be required.

(3) (U) Detailed transportation information is included in appendix X.

c. (U) Support. Provide instructions and procedures for obtaining logistics in support of GI&S missions IAW NGA and DLA procedures. Identify priorities, times required, and other necessary information.

(1) (U) External Support Procedures. This paragraph is the procedure to request crisis support from DLA or additional stockage of standard products.

(2) (U) Priority Determination. This paragraph should contain the guidance for determining support requirement priority.

UNIT	PRIORITY	DURATION	REASON

5. (U) Command and Control

a. (U) Priorities. Provide guidance for establishing command and GI&S support priorities.

b. (U) Command Relationships. Include primary and alternate locations of organic GI&S units and specify the C2 relationships among the JTF GI&S support structure and external GI&S units or agencies if not previously addressed. Refer to annex B (Intelligence) and annex J (Command Relationships) of the JTF OPORD.

c. (U) Communications and Information Systems. Reference annex K (Communications Systems) of the JTF OPORD. Identify communications information system requirements, priorities, and other pertinent information to support unit GI&S operations.

d. (U) Reports. Specify organizations and elements responsible for GI&S reports. Include the format for preparation and times, methods, and classification of submission.

Add instructions for updating maps, nautical and aeronautical charts, and digital databases. This information can be added here or in Appendix Y of this Annex.

ACKNOWLEDGE:

SIGNATURE

CLASSIFICATION

Intentionally Blank

APPENDIX D
SAMPLE APPENDIX 7 (IMAGERY INTELLIGENCE) TO ANNEX B (INTELLIGENCE)

CLASSIFICATION

CL BY

DER FROM

DECL ON

or Original classifiers of

CL BY

CL REASON

DECL ON

Copy no.   of   copies

OFFICIAL DESIGNATION OF COMMAND

PLACE OF ISSUE

Date/time group

Message reference number

APPENDIX 7 TO ANNEX B TO OPLAN ( ) INTELLIGENCE (IMAGERY)

( ) References: List applicable Director of Central Intelligence, DIA, NGA, Service, and command regulations, directives, collateral or supporting plans, studies, manuals, and estimates.

1. ( ) General

    a. ( ) Purpose. Provide general objectives and guidance necessary for accomplishing the mission.

    b. ( ) Responsibilities. Provide statement of command responsibilities, applicability and scope, and chain of command for reporting. Outline specific responsibilities of all supporting organizations and agencies. Identify IMINT roles in an all-source fusion and production environment.

2. ( ) IMINT Organizations. Identify the IMINT organizations and approximate strengths of units required.

3. ( ) Collection Activities, Functions, and Plans. For each activity or IMINT discrete function applicable to the operation, identify the staff, element, or unit responsible and the type of collection plans and approving authority required.

4. ( ) CONOPS for Imagery Collection, Processing, and Production.

    a. ( ) Refer to Appendix 1 (Priority Intelligence Requirements) and Appendix 4 (Targeting) to Annex B (Intelligence), Appendixes 1 and 9 to Annex C (Operations), and others, if applicable.

    b. ( ) Identify targets and other collection requirements to be fulfilled by IMINT operations.

    c. ( ) Obtain target and en route METOC conditions that will influence sensor selection and/or collection asset utilization. Identify both theater and national collection assets and supporting systems and how and when employed.

    d. ( ) Identify allied or coalition interface accesses and capabilities.

    e. ( ) Establish tasking procedures for standing and ad hoc IMINT requirements. Establish procedures (as required) for development, maintenance, and implementation of contingency collection problem sets or collection requirements.

    f. ( ) Identify unique logistic requirements or processes.

    g. ( ) Describe processing, exploitation, production, and dissemination operations, as well as backup procedures. Include pertinent comments on conducting imagery operations while colocated with allied or coalition forces.

    h. ( ) Summarize imagery communications requirements or reference paragraph in Annex K that states requirements.

    i. ( ) Summarize imagery systems/automated data processing requirements or reference paragraph in Annex K that states the requirements.

5. ( ) Reporting

    a. ( ) Identify reporting and dissemination needs regarding product types, timeliness for IMINT applications, capacities, and transmission media.

    b. ( ) Identify reporting dissemination procedures. Include pertinent comments on releasability and dissemination to allied or coalition forces.

6. ( ) Coordination

a. ( ) Identify coordination requirements unique to IMINT operations such as requirements identification and tasking. Refer to activities listed in paragraph 3 above, if applicable.

b. ( ) Identify coordination requirements for support.

(1) ( ) From and to other USG and allied or coalition agencies.

(2) ( ) For technical, communications, logistic, or security support.

(3) ( ) For mutual support to satisfy collection requirements. (See paragraph 3 above.)

c. ( ) Identify and/or cross-reference other imagery collection portions of the plan. For example, Annex M identifies geospatial information requirements needed to support all contemplated operations. This section should establish organizations, POCs, and procedures to ensure IMINT requirements are prioritized and tasked to support those planning and execution functions not directly related to intelligence activities.

7. ( ) Miscellaneous. Include other items not previously mentioned.

Intentionally Blank

APPENDIX E
GEOSPATIAL INTELLIGENCE REQUIREMENTS CONSIDERATIONS

1. Identify the CCMD's or JTF's GEOINT POCs. Notify subordinate forces of correct requisition procedures for predeployment topographic maps, hydrographic and aeronautical charts, and digital products.

2. Notify CCMD GEOINT cell of the GEOINT support POC in the subordinate joint force.

3. Identify subordinate joint staff GEOINT requirements to the CCMD GEOINT cell with respect to forces deploying and the operational area. Include GEOINT production quantities, personnel, and equipment to operate a map depot or digital dissemination capabilities and staff support personnel.

4. Request the following from the CCMD GEOINT cell: the production schedule; status of products and digital data required and date of first shipment; status of host-nation support for GEOINT products, digital data, and capabilities; and the status on disclosure and/or release of GEOINT to coalition forces.

5. Verify and/or submit appendix 7 (Imagery Intelligence) of annex B (Intelligence), and annex M (Geospatial Information and Services) of OPORD to J-2.

6. Request that supporting forces provide a GEOINT distribution plan. Ensure that CCMD and joint force GEOINT cells are provided a copy of all distribution plans.

7. Send a message reminding forces about accuracies, datum, and coordinates of GEOINT products and digital data. (See Appendix B, "Joint Force Intelligence Directorate Quick Reaction Checklist," in JP 2-01, *Joint and National Intelligence Support to Military Operations.*)

8. Coordinate shipment of deployment stock to the map depot. Obtain weight, physical dimensions, including cubic measurements, number of pallets, and ready-for-shipment date from DLA. Also obtain requirements for hardware, including printers and other peripheral devices, digitized mapping and charting products, and software. Forward unit line number to the CCMD GEOINT cell.

9. Identify and describe access to digital GEOINT dissemination sources.

10. Establish map depot inventory quantities to include reorder levels. Report results to the CCMD GEOINT cell via a Defense Message System message, electronic mail, or joint deployable intelligence support system.

11. Request that the CCMD GEOINT cell have NGA publish a special catalog for the operation.

12. Establish and define procedures for destruction of GEOINT products.

Intentionally Blank

APPENDIX F
GEOSPATIAL INTELLIGENCE ROLES AND RESPONSIBILITIES AND SPECIFIC GUIDANCE

1. Supported Combatant Commands

a. Maintain, within their HQ, the staff capability to direct GEOINT cell activities.

b. Appoint a GEOINT officer to lead the GEOINT cell.

c. Identify GEOINT cell members from relevant directorates and mission partners.

d. Develop appendix 7 (Imagery Intelligence), of annex B (Intelligence), and annex M (Geospatial Information and Services), IAW planning guidance contained in appendix C, "Sample Annex M (Geospatial Information and Services)," and appendix 7 (Imagery Intelligence) to annex B (Intelligence).

e. Submit requirements for GEOINT products and services IAW guidance contained in reference CJCSM 3130.03, *Adaptive Planning and Execution (APEX) Planning Formats and Guidance,* and *CJCSI 3901.01C, Requirements for Geospatial Information and Services,* and other processes (e.g., supporting GIMS and the Advanced Geospatial-Intelligence and MASINT Reporting and Dissemination Service).

f. Task components and supporting commands with mission-specific GEOINT tasks consistent with assessed capabilities (e.g., intratheater distribution, lift planning, and requirements).

g. Establish responsibilities, requirements, and procedures for the storage and maintenance of WRSs, crisis or contingency stocks, and/or directed unit holdings and allowances of GEOINT products.

h. Assess the need for and, as appropriate, request Service or NGA contingency response teams and/or NSTs to assist with GEOINT planning and operations.

i. Assess the need for, and, as appropriate, request DLA contingency support teams to assist with GEOINT planning.

j. Assess the capabilities of NSG to support operational needs. Include NSG in exercises to assess this capability. Assess NSG responsiveness to supported CCDR's needs and respond via NSG customer support teams or customer surveys.

k. Ensure intratheater connectivity exists to receive, store, and disseminate digital data.

l. Assess GEOINT readiness through the Joint Force Readiness Report.

2. Supporting Combatant Commands

a. Identify requirements for GEOINT data, information, products, and services to supported CCDRs IAW guidance contained in CJCSM 3130.03, *Adaptive Planning and Execution (APEX) Planning Formats and Guidance,* and DOD 4160.21-M, *Defense Materiel Disposition Manual.*

b. Ensure that requirements for GEOINT data, information, products, and services are included in the supported CCDR's appendix 7 (Imagery Intelligence), to annex B (Intelligence), and annex M (Geospatial Information and Services).

c. Assess the need for and, as appropriate, request Services and/or NGA contingency response teams and/or customer support teams to assist with GEOINT planning and operations.

d. Assess the need for and, as appropriate, request DLA contingency support teams and/or customer support teams to assist with GEOINT planning.

e. Assess the capability of NGA to support operational needs IAW CJCSI 3900.01C, *Position (Point and Area) Reference Procedures.* Include NGA in exercises to assess this capability. Assess NGA responsiveness to supporting CCMD needs and respond via NSTs and NGA customer surveys.

f. Assess the capability of DLA to support operational needs. Include DLA in exercises to assess this capability. Assess DLA responsiveness to supporting CCMD needs and respond via DLA customer support teams and customer surveys.

g. Establish liaison with supported command GEOINT cell.

3. Services Chiefs

a. Provide the supported CCDR with GEOINT planning factors for weapons, systems, and forces apportioned for planning. Factors include data, information, products and services, information content, format, and media.

b. Ensure forces train with the appropriate range of GEOINT data, information, products, and services.

c. Ensure that new systems are designed to use DOD-standard GEOINT data, information, products, and services where possible. Identify and submit requirements for new and unique GEOINT data, information, products, and services IAW guidance in CJCSI 3141.01D, *Management and Review of Joint Strategic Capabilities Plan (JSCP)-Tasked Plans.*

d. Ensure that logistic systems are capable of managing or requisitioning GEOINT data, information, products, and services.

e. Assess the capability of NGA to support operational needs. Include NGA in exercises to assess this capability. Assess NGA responsiveness to Service needs and respond via NSTs and customer surveys.

f. Assess the capability of DLA to support operational needs. Include DLA in exercises to assess this capability. Assess DLA responsiveness to Service needs and respond via DLA contingency support teams and customer surveys.

g. Provide information on availability of Service holdings of GEOINT data from NGA.

4. Component Commands

a. Identify requirements for GEOINT products and services to supported CCDRs IAW guidance contained in CJCSM 3130.03, *Adaptive Planning and Execution (APEX) Planning Formats and Guidance, and* CJCSI 3901.01C, *Requirements for Geospatial Information and Services.*

b. Ensure that requirements for GEOINT products and services are included in the supported CCDR's appendix 7 to annex B and annex M.

c. Develop and submit plans for intratheater distribution and stockage using the available Service logistics and communication systems.

d. Develop and submit storage and lift requirements for GEOINT products to be incorporated in the plan's TPFDD requirements.

e. Assess NGA responsiveness to component needs and respond via the operational chain-of-command. Assist the NGA CCMD NSTs and respond to customer surveys.

f. Assess DLA responsiveness to component needs and respond via the operational chain-of-command. Assist the DLA contingency support teams and respond to customer surveys.

5. National Geospatial-Intelligence Agency

a. Assist in development of GEOINT requirements to be included in appendix 7 of annex B and annex M for appropriate plans.

b. Develop support plans for all designated plans.

c. Coordinate planned production of DOD-standard GEOINT products with DLA to ensure that CCDR and Service requirements are considered when stock levels are established.

d. Train and maintain an internal crisis management team to respond to CCDR requirements.

e. Task-organize, equip, and train a deployable crisis action team to augment the CCDR's staff when requested.

f. Task-organize, equip, and train a deployable contingency response team to augment the CCDR's staff when requested. This team will deploy either with the NIST or separately upon CCMD request.

g. Produce, maintain, and participate in the distribution of maps, charts (nautical and aeronautical), target graphics, terrain analysis databases, digital products, positioning and navigation support materials and services, and related materials to support military operations and safety of navigation.

h. Disseminate or ensure the dissemination of GEOINT by the most efficient and expeditious means consistent with DOD security requirements.

i. Continue to explore the most effective means to enhance exploitation of "on demand" delivery of NGA digital information to customers to include software manipulation and remote replication capabilities.

j. Assess NGA responsiveness and readiness to support operational forces IAW CJCSI 3900.01C, *Position (Point and Area) Reference Procedures*.

k. Participate in appropriate DOD requirements and acquisition forums to ensure digital GEOINT dissemination requirements are properly identified so that DOD communications networks and infrastructures are sufficient for customer needs.

l. Develop procedures and processes to collect, archive, and disseminate user-generated GEOINT data.

m. Coordinate with the supported command's NGA support team.

6. Defense Logistics Agency

a. Serve as the DOD integrated material manager for standard GEOINT products.

b. Coordinate reprint requirements of standard GEOINT products with NGA to ensure CCDR and Service requirements can be filled in a timely manner.

c. Equip and maintain a deployable DLA support team organized to support the CCDR's staff, if requested. The team's capability should normally include the ability to support the GEOINT mission forward IAW DLA-CCDR performance-based agreements and plans.

d. Acquire, maintain inventories of, and participate in the distribution of standard maps, charts (nautical and aeronautical), air target materials, terrain analysis databases, digital products, and related materials to support military operations and safety of navigation in compliance with DOD 4160.21-M, *Defense Materiel Disposition Manual*.

e. Maintain sufficient stocks of standard GI&S products to support pre-positioned war reserve requirements and sustained crisis operation requirements IAW theater OPLAN/CONPLAN. It is incumbent for the CCMD GI&S officers to coordinate their standard GI&S requirements to ensure that DLA can have the product on the shelf. This is especially important when plans call for storing and distributing maps at one or more of DDM's nine retail MSOs; since they have limited storage capacity and personnel.

f. Establish liaison with the supported command's GEOINT cell.

Intentionally Blank

APPENDIX G
GEOSPATIAL INTELLIGENCE PRODUCTS AND SERVICES

This appendix identifies standard products, describes the product development process, and organizes the products into categories. The outline below summarizes primary data, information, products, and services produced by NGA, which have been organized into seven categories: aeronautical; nautical/hydrographic; topographical/terrestrial; precise positioning and targeting; geodesy and geophysics; geographic names; and GEOINT analysis.

1. Aeronautical Products

a. **Aim Point Graphic.** This database contains radar, infrared, and visually significant navigation and training points. It is used daily by air wings to do mission planning and operations. The Air Force Intelligence, Surveillance, and Reconnaissance Agency is a coproducer of aim point data and has the responsibility for all photographic reproductions after initial distribution.

b. **Automated Air Facilities Intelligence File.** A database on the physical characteristics of airfields, both foreign and domestic.

c. **Aeronautical Charts and Graphics.** Global and operational navigations charts, tactical pilotage charts, and joint operations graphics (JOGs).

d. **Airfield Products.** Include airfield line drawings, force protection graphics, special aeronautical information request graphics, and force protection graphic slides and airfield reports.

e. **Digital Aeronautical Flight Information File.** Consists of airports, heliports, navigation aids, waypoints, air traffic system routes, airspace boundaries, special use airspace, military training routes, parachute jump areas, and preferred routes. Used for flight planning and the programming of automated aircraft flight management systems.

f. **Digital Vertical Obstruction File.** A file consisting of man-made point features on the Earth's surface which could pose a potential hazard to flight.

g. **Electronic Chart Updating Manual.** Used for manual amendment of selected aeronautical charts with updated or corrected information pertaining to safety of air navigation.

h. **Evasion Chart.** Is designed to assist isolated personnel to evade capture and survive in hostile territory and to provide evaders with a means of navigating to a selected area for evasion or recovery. The EVC program supports operational force requirements with a series of charts that cover geographic areas specifically identified by CCMDs. The EVC is a derivative of standard products, the JOG and TLM, and is scaled at approximately 1:200,000 with map detail of approximately 1:100,000.

i. **Notice to Airmen.** Contains information concerning the establishment, condition, or change in any aeronautical facility, service, procedures, or hazard, the timely knowledge of which is essential to personnel concerned with flight operations.

j. **Flight Information Publication.** DOD planning documents, en route supplements, and terminal instrument procedures (see Figure G-1).

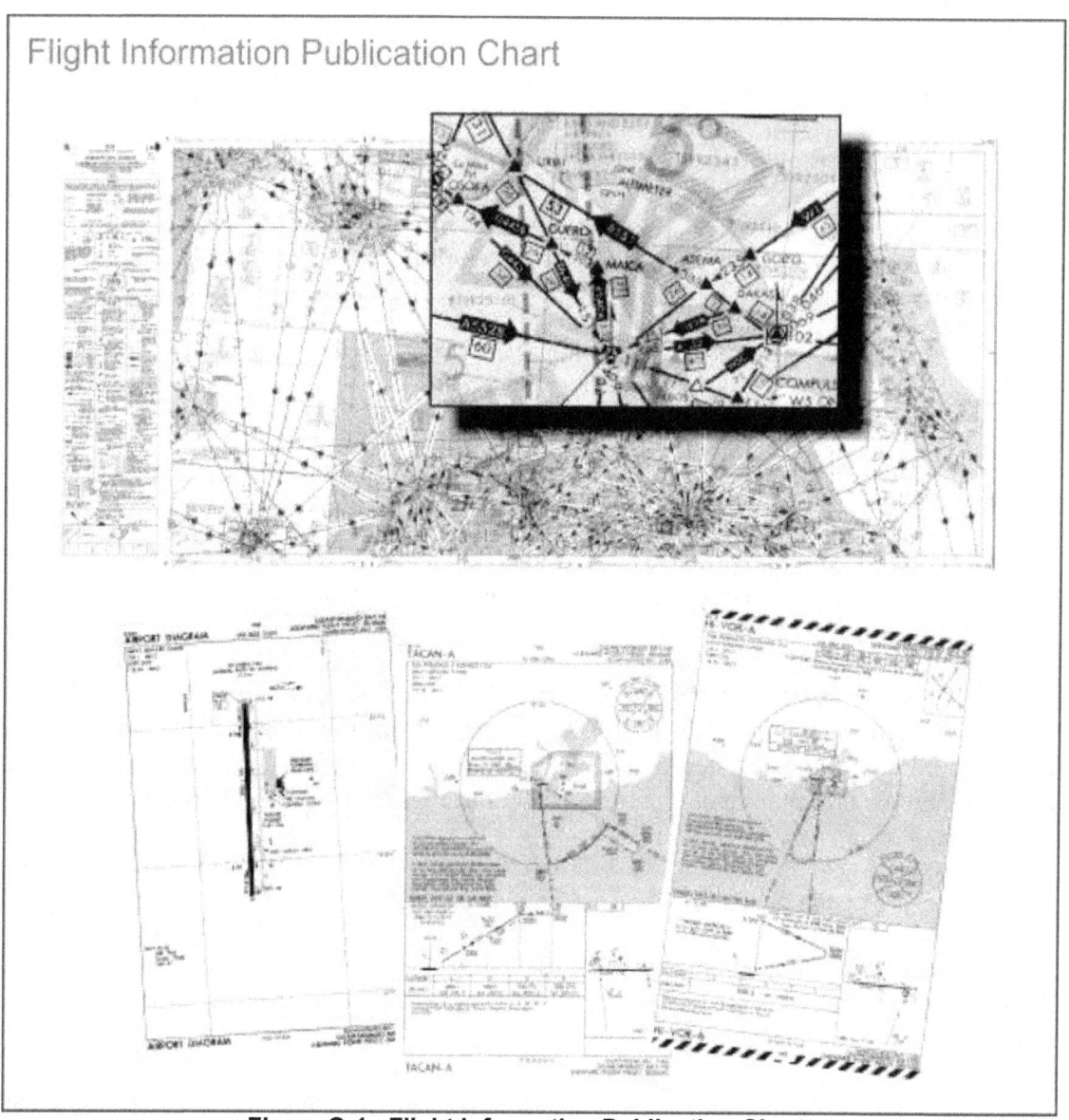

Figure G-1. Flight Information Publication Chart

2. Nautical/Hydrographic

a. **Digital Nautical Charts (DNCs).** DNCs provide worldwide databases of nautical information in vector product format. These databases are distributed via the NGA Gateway. Each DNC covers a specific geographic area of the world and consists of data partitioned into harbor, approach, coastal, and general libraries based upon the scale of the source chart. The data content and coverage closely replicate NGA's portfolio of harbor, approach, coastal, and general charts. The DNC is supported by NGA's notice to mariners.

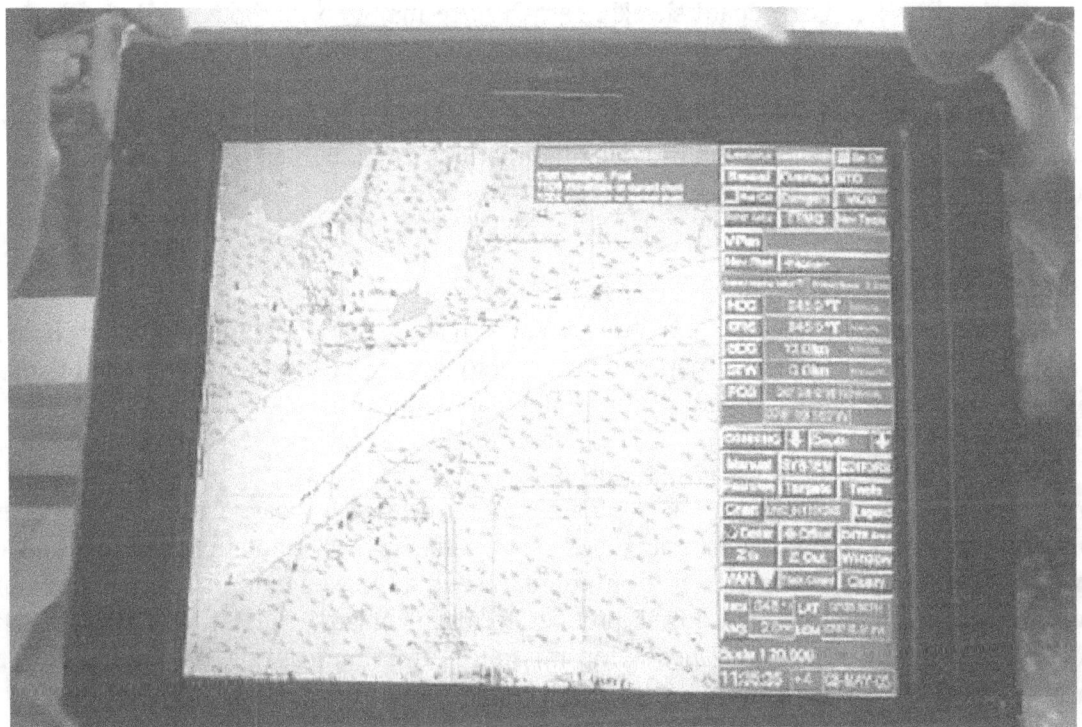

Digital nautical charts provide global nautical information.

b. **Digital Bathymetric Database.** A various-resolution gridded bathymetric database developed by the Naval Oceanographic Office (NAVOCEANO) that supports the generation of bathymetric chart products and to provide bathymetric data to be integrated with other geophysical and environmental parameters for ocean modeling.

c. **Fleet Guides.** Provide port information unique to the Navy that is not available elsewhere. Port commands contribute to the overall effectiveness by providing information related to the facilities and services available.

d. **Hydrographic Charts.** Nautical charts showing depths of water, nature of bottom, contours of bottom and coastline, and tide and currents in a given sea or sea and land area. Types of standard nautical charts include harbor, approach, coastal, and general.

e. **Tactical Ocean Data.** This product is composed of five layers that overlay DNC. These layers contain operational areas and ranges, and four submarine navigation layers.

f. **Maritime Safety Information.** Information and products required for safe navigation including charts, publications, hydrographic catalog, broadcast warning messages, mobile offshore drilling units, and anti-shipping activity messages. This data can be found on the world wide web at: http://www.nga.mil/maritime.

g. **Notice to Mariners.** Contains corrections to hardcopy hydrographic products produced by NGA, the National Ocean Service, and the USCG.

h. **Port Graphics.** Image-based products with a vector overlay of the following force protection information: seawalls, floodlights, spotlights, large light standards near/on docks, entry control points (CPs) guard shacks, hard-surface major roads, both single- and multi-lane, fence lines, and railroads.

i. **Sailing Directions.** Provide the "informational arm" to the DNC and/or standard nautical chart. Each publication provides the mariner a unique perspective by bringing to life the information graphically represented by the chart.

3. Topographical/Terrestrial

a. **Compressed ARC [Equal Arc Second Raster Chart/Map] Digitized Raster Graphic.** Scanned image of a map or chart used in any application requiring rapid display of map image or manipulation of the image of a map in raster form.

b. **Controlled Image Base.** An unclassified seamless dataset of orthophotos, usually made from grayscale images. CIB supports various weapons, theater battle management, mission planning, digital moving map displays, terrain analysis, simulation, and intelligence systems. CIB data is produced from digital source images and is compressed and reformatted to conform to the raster product format standard. CIB files are physically formatted within a National Imagery Transmission Format message. CIB may be derived from a grayscale image, from one band of a multispectral product, or from an arithmetic combination of several multispectral bands. Applications for CIB include rapid overview of areas of operations, map substitutes for emergencies and crises, metric foundation for anchoring other data in communications systems or image exploitation, positionally-correct images for draping in terrain visualization, and image backgrounds for mission planning and rehearsal.

c. **Digital Terrain Elevation Data (DTED).** A uniform matrix of terrain elevation values which provides basic quantitative data for all military systems that require terrain elevation, slope, and/or surface roughness information. DTED-formatted elevation data identified as derived from the Shuttle Radar Topography Mission is a c-band radar reflective surface offset from the ground where there is vegetation or urbanization.

d. **Topographic Line Map.** Portrays the greatest detail of topographic and cultural information in a standard view (see Figure G-2). The map is a true representation of terrain detail with relief shown by contours and spot elevations. All NGA TLM products and USGS maps have been converted to GeoPDF format.

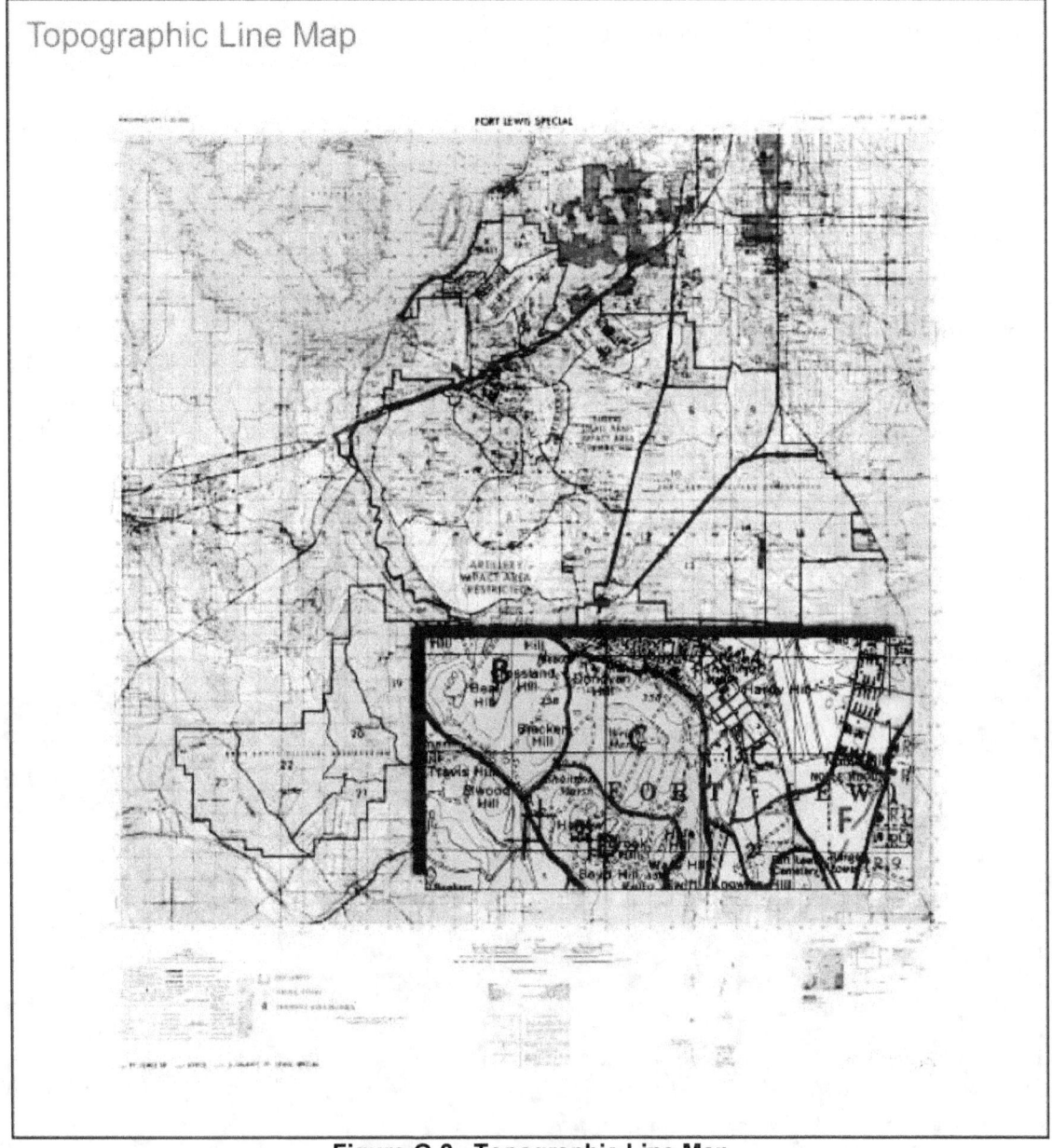

Figure G-2. Topographic Line Map

e. **Vector Feature data.** Map data consisting of points, lines, and polygons which represent natural and man-made features. Can be symbolized to provide a graphic mapping display for visualization, as well as be used to provide the geospatially referenced features and attributes necessary to conduct spatial analysis. Feature data will be compliant with the National System for Geospatial Intelligence Feature Data Dictionary family of standards and made available at the global, regional, local, and specialized/urban levels. Available in various formats to include ESRI Shapefile and Personal Geodatabase, geographic markup language, and keyhole markup language.

f. **World Mean Elevation Data.** A database of minimum, maximum, and mean terrain elevations. The preferred source is DTED. In areas with no DTED coverage, the best medium or small-scale cartographic source is used. Data collected for each 12 by 18 nautical mile cell include minimum and maximum elevation value, arithmetic mean elevation, standard deviation, source and absolute vertical accuracy.

g. **World Vector Shoreline Plus.** A digital data file containing the shorelines, international boundaries, and country names of the world. These geographic features are required for many of the digital databases being used to support geographic information systems and weapons systems.

h. **Image City Maps (ICMs).** ICMs are image-based maps of a city in either paper or digital form for close-in navigation, planning, and urban area operations.

i. **City Graphic.** A large-scale map of populated places and environs portraying streets and through-route information. It contains a numbered guide to important buildings and street names in the margin (see Figure G-3).

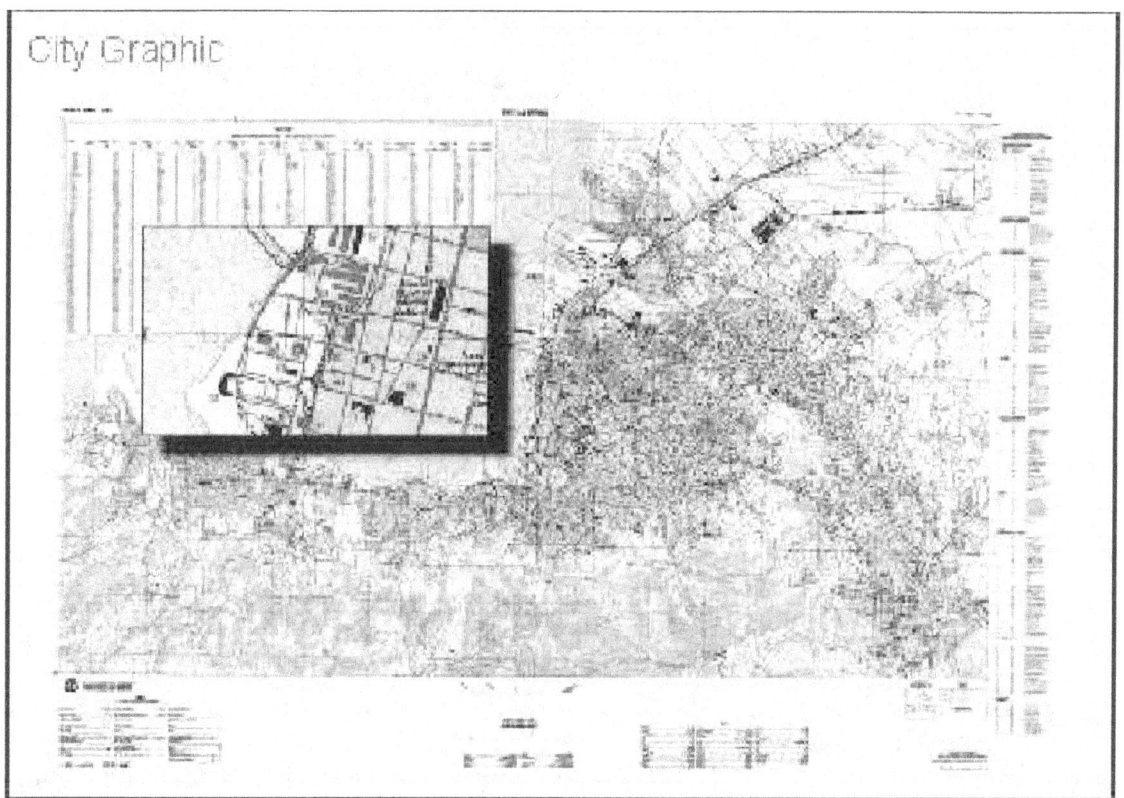

Figure G-3. City Graphic

j. **Geospatial Intelligence Base for Contingency Operations (GIBCO).** A collection of products providing coverage over specific areas designated as evacuation sites by both the Department of State and/or the unified commands. GIBCOs contain specific maps, charts, imagery, and other geospatial products to support evacuation planning and operations. GIBCOs are replacing the noncombatant evacuation operation package for each country, city, or region. The NGA produces GIBCOs, which give users flexibility through the use of Web browser technology for navigation and display of geospatial data. Applications of the GIBCO are broad, including the capability to become familiar with a foreign environment; develop a battle scene; plan, coordinate, and execute noncombatant evacuations, contingency operations, urban area missions, and search and rescue operations; as a desk-side reference; and as a means of access to geospatial data and navigation aids where networks or infrastructure have been damaged or do not exist. Tailored to each customer's request, each DVD can hold an entire country or an intensified coverage down to a single facility.

k. **Homeland Security Infrastructure Program (HSIP) Gold.** A unified compilation of USG and commercial proprietary data for homeland security uses. NGA leads the geospatial data brokering efforts called HSIP Gold. HSIP Gold serves federal-level decision makers, providing them with the geospatial information necessary to support readiness, response, and recovery planning for natural or man-made disasters.

l. **Lidar sensors** are similar to radar, transmitting laser pulses to a target and recording the time required for the pulses to return to the sensor receiver. Lidar can be used to measure shoreline and beach volume changes, shallow water depths (0-50 meters), conduct flood risk analysis, identify waterflow issues, and augment transportation mapping applications. Lidar supports large-scale production of high-resolution digital elevation products displaying accurate, highly detailed, 3-D models of structures and terrain invaluable for operational planning and mission rehearsal.

m. **Graph Plots.** A first phase line drawing of a specific target that depicts, in icon form, the order of battle found during the exploitation of that target. Generated by the Graphical Exploitation and Reporting Tool.

4. Geospatial Intelligence Targeting

a. Target materials include data supporting the COP, mission planning, precision coordinate generation, and a wide variety of analytic products and specialized data used to identify and characterize facilities at the functional level.

b. Targeting support services include validation of precision geopositioning tools and associated sensor models supporting coordinate seeking weapons, establishing minimum standards for mensuration certification and accreditation, providing a national mensuration reachback capability, and providing precision geospatial and imagery analysis and assessments in support of munitions effectiveness and target impact studies.

c. Sample targeting materials may include: Aim Point Graphic database; CIB; DPPDB; Mission Specific Data Set; terrain contour matching, terrain data (which includes

DTED, high resolution terrain elevation), and target materials supporting operational needs, analysis, and target development.

5. Geodesy

a. **Coordinate System Analysis.** Provides the parameters to transition data and products from local datums to World Geodetic System 1984 (WGS 84) and supports provision of coordinates for DOD weapons/navigation systems.

b. **Datum Transformation Parameters Metadata.** A listing of transformation parameters, solved through the systematic determination of the discrepancies between a local non-Earth centered datum and the Earth-centered WGS 84 datum.

c. **Earth Orientation Prediction Parameters.** Daily predictions of the Earth's polar position using observations from the US Naval Observatory. Predictions are published daily for each of the seven days beginning with Sunday of each week.

d. **Geodetic Surveys.** NGA executes geodetic surveys worldwide in support of US national interests. State-of-the-art techniques are used to collect, process, and analyze data. Survey types include geodetic, astronomic, gravity, gradiometry, terminal aeronautical global navigation satellite system geodetic (airfield), and hand-held GEOINT (stills and immersive).

e. **GPS Precise Ephemeris.** DOD truth for GPS orbits. Computed after the fact for best accuracy, used for precise positioning and WGS 84 reference frame.

f. **GPS Monitor Station Data.** NGA provides its global GPS network data to the USAF for inclusion in their GPS mission. Used for GPS precise ephemeris.

g. **GPS Situational Awareness.** Can include GPS interference information, availability, and accuracy.

h. **Deflection of the Vertical.** This gravity data is essential to the accuracy and effectiveness of high order inertial navigation systems (INSs) as it reduces position and velocity errors and improves orientation control when used as part of the INS solution. If left uncompensated, the largest errors in an INS are induced by variations in the Earth's gravity field.

i. **Geotechnical Analysis.** Developing and generating models and products to characterize the properties and composition of the surface and near-subsurface of the Earth. Applications include: hydrologic modeling for a country-wide surface drainage network. Soil characterization based on physical and geochemical traits. Flood potential modeling to delineate and rank areas based on its susceptibility to flooding.

6. Geographic Names

a. **Federal Information Processing Standards Publication 10-4.** Provides a list of the basic geopolitical entities in the world, together with the principal administrative divisions to comprise each entity.

b. **Foreign Names Information Bulletin.** Provides up-to-date information regarding the place-name decisions of the Foreign Names Committee of the US Board on Geographic Names. The bulletin is issued electronically on a quarterly basis.

c. **US Board on Geographic Names.** The interagency board established by public law to standardize geographic name spellings for use in government publications.

d. **Geographic Net Names Server.** Provides access to NGA's and the US Board on Geographic Names' database of foreign geographic feature names.

7. Geospatial Intelligence Analysis

a. **Baseline Reports.** Intelligence and information products consisting of text and graphics produced by image analysts to establish a snapshot of historic events of the region/facility of interest. These reports are then compared by analysts to determine the progress of specific events or situations such as the construction of nuclear power plants or the effects of local strikes by the work force on an industrial facility.

b. **Cables.** Highlight and intelligence problem cables. Message traffic used to disseminate any high-interest or time-sensitive events/activities observed on imagery to the rest of the IC. The information contained in these cables is generally processed by image analysts within moments of the images being downloaded.

c. **Facility Products.** Collected intelligence-related materials such as images, reference images, reports, text, maps, and sketches on a specific subject or facility.

d. **First Looks.** Annotated image graphics and text that present events/activity observed on imagery by the NGA current operations analysts. These products represent the first reporting of an observed activity and precede the National Geospatial-Intelligence Agency intelligence brief.

e. **Imagery Derived Products (IDPs).** Any representation made from US classified satellite imagery that is not a direct copy of the original image itself. IDPs can either be literal or nonliteral representations. Literal IDPs are image-like products (e.g., panchromatic images), while nonliteral IDPs are graphic products such as maps, line drawings, or graphs and statistical data derived from imagery. IDPs can be in hard or softcopy form. The IDP program is managed by NGA on behalf of the DNI. The program is designed to manage and support the generation of IDPs where a compelling and justifiable requirement exists to disclose or release an image or imagery-derived information to persons without security clearances (such as public briefings, field personnel, contractors, state or local agencies, as well as foreign nationals as part of a coalition) and no practical alternative exists.

f. **Intelligence and Information Reports.** Cover a wide range of formats including intelligence summaries, intelligence information reports, research papers, reference aids, intelligence assessments, chronologies, blind memoranda, situation reports, tactical action reports, handbooks, sanctions monitoring reports, imagery maps, tabular material, and graphics presentations.

g. **NGA Intelligence Brief.** A set of annotated graphics of a current event with some attached explanatory text.

h. **NGA Morning Intelligence Summaries.** An executive-style update intended for policymakers and senior IC officials. It provides a synopsis of significant IMINT produced over the last 24 hours and highlights collection initiatives and relevant negative reporting on issues of high current interest.

8. **Computer Uniform Resource Locators**

Detailed information and descriptions on products and services can be found at the following uniform resource locators unless otherwise listed:

a. **Army Geospatial Enterprise Products**

(1) Army full-spectrum GEOINT provides products through the GETS. Production may also be requested through this web portal. (JWICS link: www.amrds.geoint.ic.gov. SIPRNET link: www.amrds.agi.nga.smil.mil)

(2) US Army Geospatial Center link. (www.tec.army.smil.mil and www.agc.army.mil)

b. **Marine Corps Intelligence Activity.** MCIA provides tailored intelligence and services to the Marine Corps, the other Services, and the IC based on expeditionary mission profiles in littoral areas. MCIA supports the development of Service doctrine, force structure, training and education, and acquisition. (Classified http://www.mcia.usmc.smil.mil)

c. **Navy Products**

(1) Unclassified METOC: Naval Enterprise Portal-Oceanography. NIPRNET home page. (https://nepoc.oceanography.navy.mil)

(2) Classified: METOC: Naval Enterprise Portal-Oceanography. SIPRNET home page contains links to products. (http://nepoc.oceanography.navy.smil.mil)

(3) **JWICS**

(a) Office of Naval Intelligence Maritime Intelligence Portal. (http://144.238.238.20/servlet/page?_pageid=80,86&_dad=portal30&_schema=PORTAL30)

(b) Office of Naval Intelligence Imagery Operations Department. (http://northstar.nmic.ic.gov/onihome/intelloperations/imageryoperations/index.htm)

(c) Oceanography: NAVOCEANO JWICS Home Page. (http://www.navo.ic.gov)

(d) Meteorology: Fleet Numerical Meteorology and Oceanography Center (FNMOC) JWICS Home Page. (http://www.fnmoc.ic.gov)

(4) Naval Pacific METOC Center/Joint Typhoon Warning Center Home Page. (http://phmetoc.pacom.ic.gov)

d. **Air Force Products and Services**

(1) **National Air and Space Intelligence Center**

(a) JWICS: http://www.naic.ic.gov/img for imagery-derived products, http://www.naic.ic.gov/masint for AGI products, and http://www.dibportal.ds.naic.ic.gov/DGS%20NASIC/ for access to multiple intelligence discipline support to military operations

(b) SIPRNET: http://www.naic.wrightpatterson.af.smil.mil/geoint and http://dibportal.afmc.af.smil.mil/DGS%20NASIC/

(2) **480th ISR Wing.** SIPRNET: http://intelink.480iw.langley.af.smil.mil

(3) **Air Force Targeting Center.** SIPRNET: http://aftc.langley.af.smil.mil

(4) **GPS Operations Center.** SIPRNET: http://gpsoc1.afspc.smil.mil

e. **NGA Products**

(1) Maritime Safety and Navigation. (Unclassified: http://pollux.nss.nga.mil)

(2) NIPRNET: https://www.geointel.nga.mil/ or https://www.extranet.nga.mil

(3) NGA Homepage contains links/menus for GEOINT products and services. (Classified: http://www.nga.smil.mil/products.html and unclassified: https://www.geointel.nga.mil/)

(4) **JWICS**

(a) List of all NGA products with a description of each. (http://www.stl.nga.ic.gov/products/productdesc/listall.cfm)

(b) Alphabetical list of GEOINT services and products, with links. (http://www.nga.ic.gov)

f. **USNORTHCOM Products—JWICS**

(1) North American Aerospace Defense Command USNORTHCOM GEOINT Products. This is the USNORTHCOM home page, which provides information on homeland security and disaster relief. (http://www.northcom.ic.gov/DP04/geoint.html)

(2) This site provides information on a variety of links that contain GEOINT information and products related to North America. (http://www.northcom.ic.gov/geoint.html)

g. **USCG Products**

(1) JWICS: http://intellipedia.intelink.ic.gov/wiki/Intelligence_Coordination_Center_GEOINT_Branch

(2) SIPRNET: http://www.intelink.sgov.gov/wiki/ICC_GEOINT_Branch and: http://www.icc.uscg.smil.mil/GEOINT.cfm?isJWICS=

(3) Unclassified: https://www.intelink.gov/wiki/ICC_GEOINT_Branch

APPENDIX H
GEOSPATIAL DATUMS AND COORDINATE REFERENCE SYSTEMS

1. Position Reference Procedures

a. WGS 84 is the official DOD positional reference system. IAW CJCSI 3900.01, *Position (Point and Area) Reference Procedures,* in unilateral and joint operations, the US military force of the commander involved will use the WGS 84 horizontal coordinates and height (height above ellipsoid) unless the commander determines that the use of other position reference systems (i.e., horizontal and/or vertical datum) is mission critical. Universal use of the WGS 84 position reference system (datum) will eliminate confusion regarding which system is being used in reporting positions. Only ellipsoidal heights from approved sources should be used to support precision targeting with coordinate seeking weapons. The two coordinate reference systems to be used for reporting and referencing positions (referenced to WGS 84) shall be:

(1) Geographic coordinates using the sexagesimal system, expressed (represented) in degrees, minutes, and decimal minutes (DDMM.mmmm).

(2) **The Military Grid Reference System (MGRS).** Ground units and ground combat operations shall be serviced with MGRS coordinates. To support homeland security and homeland defense, the federal Geographic Data Committee US National Grid standard when referenced to North American Datum 1983 (NAD 83) is operationally equivalent to and is an accepted substitute for MGRS coordinates referenced to WGS 84. Note that at mapping scales of 1:5000 and smaller, NAD 83, and WGS 84 are considered equivalent.

b. In all joint operations, users will reference coordinates (horizontal and vertical) to WGS 84. Due to WGS 84's global 3-D datum characteristics, and because several vertical models are defined within WGS 84, users will report the vertical model referenced (e.g., Earth Gravity Model [EGM] 2008, EGM 96, EGM 08), whenever a deviation of the policy stated becomes necessary. If some preexisting circumstance precludes using the WGS 84 datum or any of its components (horizontal, vertical, or both), CCDRs will coordinate on the position reference system(s) (horizontal and/or vertical datum) and procedures to be used.

c. For any operation, several local and/or regional horizontal and vertical datums may exist throughout an AOI and, under special circumstances, may be used in lieu of WGS 84. CCDRs will determine the appropriate local and/or regional horizontal and/or vertical reference system (datum) for use, and coordinate with the National Geospatial-Intelligence Agency (NGA/Office of Geomatics or Office of the Director of Military Support) for technical advice. The conditions for use of local datums and any limitations or restrictions will be published in annex M of applicable plans and orders. Furthermore, due to the existence of several vertical datums worldwide from which to derive heights—with each height modeling a different surface (e.g., ellipsoid, geoid, and topographic)—extreme care must be exercised when reporting the vertical coordinate of a 3-D position. As a result, users will report the height source and vertical datum IAW the procedures contained in the enclosure to CJCSI 3900.01C, *Position (Point and Area) Reference Procedures.* This does not preclude the use of other coordinate formats to support intelligence databases, target materials, and ISR applications.

d. Two-dimensional (2-D) point positional information shall be represented as either geographic coordinates or grid coordinates. When reporting 2-D positional information using geographic coordinates, use the sexagesimal system, expressed or represented in degrees, minutes, and decimal minutes (DDMM.mmmm). When reporting 2-D point positional information using grid coordinates, and unless otherwise directed by the respective CCDR, use the universal transverse mercator or universal polar stereographic grid system, expressed in the grid reference alphanumeric position reporting system, MGRS.

e. Express the vertical component as either a positive (+), to indicate that the position is above the vertical datum, or a negative (-), to indicate that the position is below the vertical datum, and identify the unit of measure.

f. All graphical 2-D and 3-D positional data software shall simultaneously display geographic and MGRS coordinates IAW the above except where miniaturization of system displays renders this impractical.

2. Area Reference Procedures

a. In multinational and joint operations, CCDRs should direct the use of the Global Area Reference System (GARS) unless the commander determines that the use of another area reference system (e.g., locally developed area reference systems such as the Korean common grid reference system) is mission critical. Universal use of the GARS area reference system will eliminate confusion regarding which system is being used in reporting areas.

b. GARS is primarily an operational-level administrative measure used to coordinate geographic areas rapidly for operational environment deconfliction and synchronization of operations. It provides a common language between the Services and components. GARS is not a replacement for position-reference procedures or systems described above. It is not used to describe exact geographic locations or to express precise positions for guided weapon employment, or to describe areas smaller than five minutes by five minutes.

c. GARS is a reference system, not a fire support coordination measure (FSCM) or airspace coordinating measure (ACM). It provides the 2-D construction from which control and coordination measures can be constructed. Such control measures include FSCMs, ACMs, joint special operations areas, no-fly areas, and maritime control measures to name several. The area reference system can be used for a variety of purposes to include identification of littoral maritime warfare areas for antisubmarine warfare and antisurface warfare forces. The area reference system can be a tool for rapid deconfliction within the operational environment.

d. The GARS system uses three numbers followed by two letters to describe a unique 30 minute by 30 minute area. A graphical depiction is in Figure H-1. The origin point for the system is 90 degrees south (the South Pole) and 180 degrees east/west. The areas described by GARS are coincident with even WGS 84 degree and minute lines. The areas

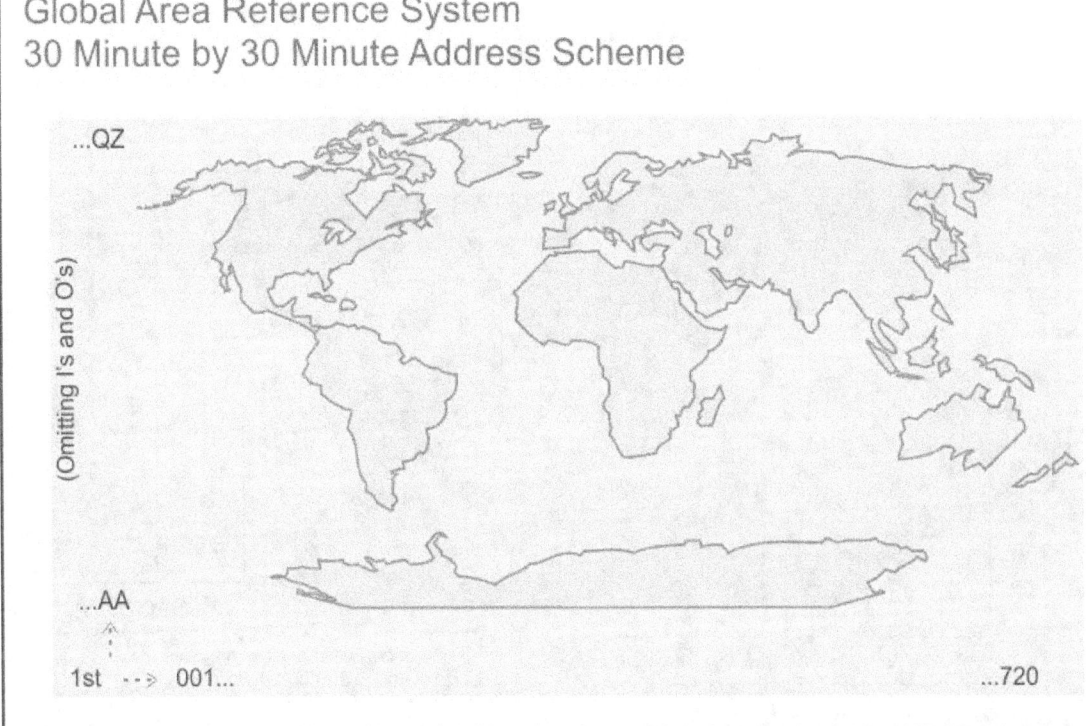

Global Area Reference System
30 Minute by 30 Minute Address Scheme

...QZ

(Omitting I's and O's)

...AA

1st --> 001...   ...720

Figure H-1. Global Area Reference System 30 Minute by 30 Minute Address Scheme

are read right (west to east, 001-720) then up (south to north, AA-QZ). The 30 minute by 30 minute areas are subdivided by quadrant into 15 minute by 15 minute areas, then further subdivided by a keypad division into 5 minute by 5 minute areas (see Figure H-2).

3. Point Reference Systems

a. Point references complement area references by providing a multitude of common surface points to expedite coordination throughout the JOA. The point reference system is similar to the area reference system in that it can be used to provide components with a common perspective of the battlespace and allow for common identification of mutually accessible attack areas. In addition, it can be used to identify the center point for the establishment of an appropriate FSCM and/or ACM.

(1) **Bullseye and Search and Rescue Point (SARDOT).** The bullseye reference system is normally used during counterair engagements for SA on targeted and untargeted airborne threats and for other coordination. Normally, theaters will only establish a few bullseye reference points to ensure effectiveness. Bullseyes are not meant to provide detailed target guidance, but general reference information. SARDOTs, like bullseyes, are very few in number and provide general area reference for search and rescue operations.

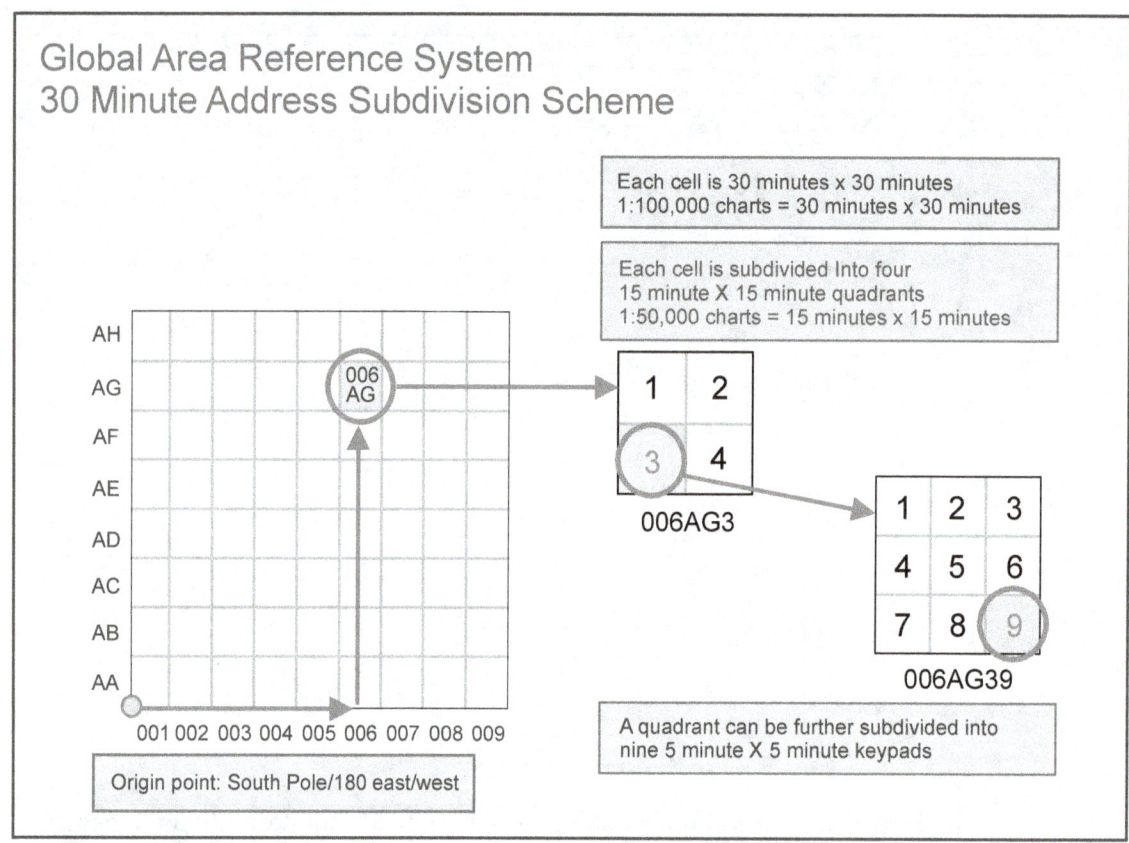

Figure H-2. Global Area Reference System 30 Minute Address Subdivision Scheme

(2) **CPs and Initial Points (IPs).** Theaters establish CPs and IPs to enable rapid and accurate geolocation information for joint operations. As opposed to only a few bullseye points, CPs and IPs are established throughout the theater and their effectiveness increases with promulgation. CPs and IPs provide the references for operations that require significant accuracy, such as targeting guidance. As such, they are the point reference system of choice for air-ground integration during close air support.

(3) **US Army Terrain Index Reference System and Target Reference Point.** These point reference systems are developed for surface component operations to quickly identify a target off a known geographic point. They differ from CPs and IPs in that they are primarily for surface unit coordination, not component coordination. As such, they are nominated and distributed more rapidly among surface units without further promulgation and coordination of the joint force.

b. **Point Reference System Design.** The JFC or designated representative establishes a CP and/or IP point system throughout the operational area by selecting geographic points of reference and encoding them alphanumerically or with code words. These geographic points will be incorporated into operational graphics and overlays of component C2 systems, such as Advanced Field Artillery Tactical Data System, Theater Battle Management Core System, Airborne Element Tactical Air Control System databases, and the airspace control plan.

c. **Point Reference Execution.** When only general area reference is required, bullseyes may be referenced. Examples include air-to-air threat information and SARDOTs for combat search and rescue coordination. When accuracy is required for component integration, such as target identification, CPs and IPs should be referenced. A target's azimuth and distance from a selected CP or IP can provide effective coordination.

4. Coordination

a. The Director, NGA, will establish specifications and procedures for applying position reference systems to GEOINT. WGS 84 is the official DOD position reference system. NGA will assist its allied coproducers in using this system. When WGS 84 cannot be used, NGA will assist the CCDRs in determining an appropriate reference system. NGA will provide standard algorithms and parameters to perform datum transformation and coordinate conversion (e.g., as implemented in Geographic Translator or Mensuration Services Program). For existing products (e.g., maps, software, aircraft systems) not in compliance with this instruction, NGA will coordinate with the affected agency, CCDR, or Service on the feasibility of converting these products with regard to time, cost, and scheduling. NGA will coordinate with the Joint Staff, DOD agencies, CCMDs, and the Services in making all future products used for position reference in compliance with this instruction.

b. CCDRs will develop procedures for coordinating the use of the WGS 84 system of coordinates in all joint operations involving US military forces. CCDRs will coordinate with allied or coalition commands on position reference procedures to be followed within areas of multinational interest. In cases where conditions preclude the use of WGS 84, CCDRs will coordinate on the use of position reference procedures. Examples of the authorized reference system formats are provided in Figure H-3.

Examples of Authorized Reference System Formats

Geographic coordinates	3659.9390N 10902.7100W
Military grid reference system	12SXF7394596545
Global Area Reference System	142LP23

Figure H-3. Examples of Authorized Reference System Formats

Intentionally Blank

APPENDIX J
METEOROLOGICAL AND OCEANOGRAPHIC SUPPORT TO GEOSPATIAL INTELLIGENCE

1. Relationship of Meteorological and Oceanographic to Geospatial Intelligence

As shown in NSG Basic Doctrine Publication 1-0, *Geospatial Intelligence (GEOINT) Basic Doctrine,* as a value-added partner, METOC data complements and enhances the GEOINT information base. METOC conditions can affect other GEOINT activities, so a detailed understanding of the operational environment, both in the planning process and during ongoing operations, is critical to joint operations.

2. Meteorological and Oceanographic Doctrine

METOC operations are described in detail in JP 3-59, *Meteorological and Oceanographic Operations*, and CJCSI 3810.01C, *Meteorological and Oceanographic Operations.* METOC responsibility is normally assigned to the J-3, but may be assigned to J-2 if the commander desires (typical where an Army organization is assigned as the lead element). The joint meteorological and oceanographic officer (JMO) is the primary METOC point of POC for obtaining METOC information. The JMO operates within theater guidance provided by the senior METOC officer.

3. National System for Geospatial Intelligence Meteorological and Oceanographic Specialty Team

The GEOINT functional manager designated an NSG senior meteorological and oceanographic officer (SMO) to provide centralized coordination for METOC activities affecting GEOINT across the NSG. The NSG SMO instituted the meteorological and oceanographic Specialty Team program to integrate METOC personnel into the intelligence operations centers to provide dedicated and tailored support. A link to their product website can be found here: JWICS: http://www.intelink.ic.gov/wiki/ADF-E_METOC.

4. Theater Meteorological and Oceanographic Guidance

The CCMD SMO is responsible for setting METOC policy in the GCC's AOR, normally through a METOC OPORD/OPLAN/CONPLAN annex H. All SMOs are currently assigned to J-3, but support all directorates and components. The CCMD METOC SIPRNET sites containing theater policy and standardized products for operational use are listed below:

a. United States Central Command (USCENTCOM): http://hqsweb03.centcom.smil.mil/index.asp?division=ccj3-ow&stat=o/

b. United States European Command (USEUCOM): http://www.eucom.smil.mil/subpage/metoc.htm/

c. USNORTHCOM: https://https://operations.noradnorthcom.smil.mil/sites/battlest aff/dsca/metoc/

    d. USPACOM:
http://https://psp.hq.pacom.smil.mil/orgareas/j3/j33/j331/j3319/pages/

    e. United States Southern Command (USSOUTHCOM):
http:// https://scportalanon.suthcom.smil.mil/DIRandLNOs/j3/j33/metoc/

    f. USSTRATCOM: https://scie.stratcom.smil.mil/sites/SGS/J3-4/J33/j302/default.aspx

    g. USTRANSCOM: https://www.transcom.smil.mil/j3/mcc/wx/metoc_home.html

    h. CJCS: http://c2www.af.pentagon.smil.mil/afog/wx/

5. Climatology Support for Planning

During the planning process, climatology or historical weather data for the AOI can be obtained through the SMO, JMO, or staff weather officer. If no METOC officer is assigned, climatology data can be obtained from the 14th Weather Squadron (WS), FNMOC, or the National Climatic Data Center (NCDC). Historical and climatological oceanographic information can be obtained from the NAVOCEANO. Links to the climatology centers can be found here:

    a. 14th WS:

        NIPRNET: https://notus2.afccc.af.mil/SCIS/

        SIPRNET: http://siprweb2.asheville.af.smil.mil/SCIS

        JWICS: http://www.afccc.ic.gov/SCIS/

    b. FNMOC:

        NIPRNET: https://portal.fnmoc.navy.mil/climatology/cgi-bin/climoRequest.cgi

        SIPRNET: http://portal.fnmoc.navy.smil.mil/climatology/cgi-bin/climoRequest.cgi

    c. NCDC:

        NIPRNET: http://lwf.ncdc.noaa.gov/oa/ncdc.html

    d. NAVOCEANO:

        NIPRNET: https://nepoc.oceanography.navy.mil

        SIPRNET: http://nepoc.oceanography.navy.smil.mil

6. Real-Time Meteorological and Oceanographic Support and Data

Real-time METOC support and data support for the GEOINT process can be obtained through METOC applications on various systems, and through unclassified and unclassified websites. Soil moisture from weather satellites is relayed through these METOC systems for applications to trafficability and other intelligence preparation of the operational environment processes. METOC information from civilian and foreign sites is widely available, but non-DOD data can be suspect and is not consistently available. Per CJCSI 3810.01C, *Meteorological and Oceanographic Operations*, civilian and foreign METOC sources should not be used for operational purposes without being approved by the SMO or JMO. When a JMO is not assigned, Service production centers can receive and respond to requests for real-time, tailored METOC support within their respective area of forecast responsibility. Navy and Air Force METOC production centers and regional METOC agencies provide dynamic real-time support to operating forces.

a. **Air Force METOC Centers**

(1) AFWA is the main METOC production center for Army and Air Force weather and all Service space weather information. Links to AFWA services can be found here:

(a) Air Force Weather-Web Services (geographic information system-based visualization interface).

<u>1</u>. NIPRNET: https://weather.af.mil

<u>2</u>. SIPRNET: http://weather.af.smil.mil

<u>3</u>. JWICS: http://afwwebs.weather.ic.gov

(b) JAAWIN [Joint Air Force and Army Weather Information Network] (legacy visualization interface)

<u>1</u>. NIPRNET: https://weather.afwa.af.mil

<u>2</u>. SIPRNET: http://safwin.offutt.af.smil.mil

<u>3</u>. JWICS: http://jafwin.afwa.ic.gov/

(c) AFWA Operations Center:

<u>1</u>. NIPRNET: AFWAOperationsCenter@offutt.af.mil

<u>2</u>. SIPRNET: AFWAOperationsCenter@offutt.af.smil.mil

<u>3</u>. Defense Switched Network (DSN): 271-2586

(2) Operational weather squadrons (OWSs) are regional USAF METOC centers. Links to them by region are as follows:

(a) 17 OWS (USPACOM)

1. NIPRNET: https://17ows.hickam.af.mil/

2. SIPRNET: http://17ows.hickam.af.smil.mil/

3. DSN: 315-449-8335

(b) 21 OWS (United States Africa Command [USAFRICOM]/USEUCOM)

1. NIPRNET: https://ows.sembach.af.mil/

2. SIPRNET: http://ows.usafe.af.smil.mil/

3. DSN: 314-489-2136

(c) 23 OWS (USSOCOM)

1. NIPRNET: https://23ws.hurlburt.af.mil/

2. SIPRNET: http://23ws.afsoc.af.smil.mil/

3. DSN: 579-4348

(d) 28 OWS (USCENTCOM)

1. NIPRNET: https://28ows.shaw.af.mil

2. SIPRNET: https://ows.sc.afcent.af.smil.mil/

3. DSN: 965-0489

(e) 612 Operational Weather Flight (USSOUTHCOM)

1. NIPRNET: https://25ows.dm.af.mil/

2. SIPRNET: http://25ows.davismonthan.af.smil.mil/

3. DSN: 228-1977

(f) 15 OWS (USNORTHCOM, NE/NC continental United States [CONUS]/E Canada)

1. NIPRNET: https://ows.scott.af.mil/

2. SIPRNET: https://ows.scott.af.smil.mil/

<u>3.</u> DSN: 576-9699

(g) 25 OWS (USNORTHCOM, W CONUS/W Canada)

<u>1.</u> NIPRNET: https://25ows.dm.af.mil/

<u>2.</u> SIPRNET: https://25ows.dm.af.smil.mil/

<u>3.</u> DSN: 228-7655

(h) 26 OWS (USNORTHCOM, SE/SC CONUS/Mexico)

<u>1.</u> NIPRNET: https://ows.barksdale.af.mil/

<u>2.</u> SIPRNET: https://ows.barksdale.af.smil.mil/

<u>3.</u> DSN: 331-2600

b. **Navy METOC Centers**

(1) Fleet Numerical METOC Center, Monterey, CA is the main METOC production center for Navy and Marine Corps weather information. Links to other Navy oceanography information are:

(a) NIPRNET: https://www.fnmoc.navy.mil (http://nepoc.oceanography.navy.mil)

(b) SIPRNET: http://www.fnmoc.navy.smil.mil http://nepoc.oceanography.navy.smil.mil/

(c) JWICS: http://www.fnmoc.ic.gov

(2) NAVOCEANO, Stennis Space Center, MS, which hosts the Warfighting Support Center, is the main DOD production site for oceanographic and riverine METOC information. Links to Navy regional METOC centers are:

(a) NIPRNET: https://www.navo.navy.mil https://nepoc.oceanography.navy.mil

(b) SIPRNET: http://www.navo.navy.smil.mil http://nepoc.oceanography.navy.smil.mil

(c) JWICS: http://www.navo.ic.gov/

(3) Navy METOC Enterprise. Navy and Marine Corps oriented support can be attained by contacting the Navy METOC enterprise watch (Primary) or the fleet weather centers (FWCs) (Alternates) at:

(a) Commander, Naval Meteorology and Oceanography Command (CNMOC) Oceanography Operational Watch (Global).

1. CNMOC Oceanographic Operations Watch (COOW): COOW.fct@navy.mil.

2. COOW_SIPR.fct@navy.smil.mil

3. NIPRNET: https://nepoc.oceanography.navy.mil/

4. SIPRNET: http://nepoc.oceanography.navy.smil.mil/

5. DSN: 312-828-4019

(b) FWC Norfolk, VA (USNORTHCOM [East CONUS, Gulf of Mexico], USEUCOM, USSOUTHCOM, USAFRICOM).

1. NIPRNET: https://nepoc.oceanography.navy.mil/

2. SIPRNET: http://nepoc.oceanography.navy.smil.mil/

3. DSN: 312-836-7750

(c) FWC San Diego, CA (USNORTHCOM [West CONUS, Alaska], USPACOM, USCENTCOM).

1. NIPRNET: https://nepoc.oceanography.navy.mil/

2. SIPRNET: http://nepoc.oceanography.navy.smil.mil/

3. DSN: 312-735-1271

APPENDIX K
REFERENCES

The development of JP 2-03 is based upon the following primary references:

1. Department of Defense Publications

a. DOD Directive 3025.18, *Defense Support of Civil Authorities.*

b. DOD Directive 5105.60, *National Geospatial-Intelligence Agency (NGA).*

c. DOD Directive 5230.11, *Disclosure of Classified Military Information to Foreign Governments and International Organizations.*

d. DOD 5240.1-R, *Procedures Governing the Activities of DOD Intelligence Components that Affect United States Persons.*

e. DOD Instruction 5000.56, *Programming Geospatial Intelligence (GEOINT), Geospatial Information and Services (GI&S), and Geodesy Requirements for Developing Systems.*

f. DOD 4160.21-M, *Defense Material Disposition Manual.*

g. DOD 5200.1-PH, *DOD Guide to Marking Classified Documents.*

h. DOD *Electronic Foreign Clearance Guide.*

2. Chairman of the Joint Chiefs of Staff Publications

a. CJCSI 3110.08D, *Geospatial Information and Services Supplemental Instruction to Joint Strategic Capabilities Plan (JSCP).*

b. CJCSI 3141.01E, *Management and Review of Joint Strategic Capabilities Plan (JSCP)- Tasked.*

c. CJCSI 3810.01C, *Meteorological and Oceanographic Operations.*

d. CJCSI 3900.01C, *Position (Point and Area) Reference Procedures.*

e. CJCSI 3901.01C, *Requirements for Geospatial Information and Services.*

f. CJCSI 5120.02C, *Joint Doctrine Development System.*

g. CJCSI 6130.01, *Master Positioning, Navigation and Timing Plan.*

h. CJCSM 3130.03, *Adaptive Planning and Execution (APEX) Planning Formats and Guidance.*

i. JP 1, *Doctrine for the Armed Forces of the United States.*

j JP 1-02, *Department of Defense Dictionary of Military and Associated Terms.*

k. JP 2-0, *Joint Intelligence.*

l. JP 2-01, *Joint and National Intelligence Support to Military Operations.*

m. JP 3-0, *Joint Operations.*

n. JP 3-27, *Homeland Defense.*

o. JP 3-28, *Defense Support of Civil Authorities.*

p. JP 3-34, *Joint Engineer Operations.*

q. JP 3-59, *Meteorological and Oceanographic Operations.*

r. JP 4-0, *Joint Logistics.*

s. JP 4-09, *Distribution Operations.*

t. JP 5-0, *Joint Operation Planning.*

u. JP 6-0, *Joint Communications System.*

3. Other Publications

a. Military Handbook 850, *Glossary of Mapping, Charting, and Geodetic Terms.*

b. NSG Publication 1-0, *Geospatial Intelligence (GEOINT) Basic Doctrine.*

c. NGA Technical Manual 8358.1, *Datum, Ellipsoids, Grids, and Grid Reference Systems.*

d. NGA Technical Manual 8358.2, *The Universal Grids: Universal Transverse Mercator (UTM) and Universal Polar Stereographic (UPS).*

e. NGA Technical Reference 8350.2, *The DOD World Geodetic System 1984.*

APPENDIX L
ADMINISTRATIVE INSTRUCTIONS

1. User Comments

Users in the field are highly encouraged to submit comments on this publication to: the Joint Staff Directorate for Joint Force Development (J-7), Deputy Director, Joint and Coalition Warfighting, Joint and Coalition Warfighting Center, ATTN: Joint Doctrine Support Division, 116 Lake View Parkway, Suffolk, VA 23435-2697. These comments should address content (accuracy, usefulness, consistency, and organization), writing, and appearance.

2. Authorship

The lead agent for this publication is the Joint Staff J-7, and the primary review authority is the National Geospatial-Intelligence Agency. The Joint Staff doctrine sponsor for this publication is the Director for Intelligence (J-2).

3. Supersession

This publication supersedes JP 2-03, 22 March 2007, *Geospatial Intelligence Support to Joint Operations*.

4. Change Recommendations

a. Recommendations for urgent changes to this publication should be submitted:

TO: JOINT STAFF WASHINGTON DC//J7-JEDD//

b. Routine changes should be submitted electronically to the Deputy Director, Joint and Coalition Warfighting, Joint and Coalition Warfighting Center, Joint Doctrine Support Division and info the lead agent and the Director for Joint Force Development, J-7/JEDD.

c. When a Joint Staff directorate submits a proposal to the CJCS that would change source document information reflected in this publication, that directorate will include a proposed change to this publication as an enclosure to its proposal. The Services and other organizations are requested to notify the Joint Staff J-7 when changes to source documents reflected in this publication are initiated.

5. Distribution of Publications

Local reproduction is authorized, and access to unclassified publications is unrestricted. However, access to, and reproduction authorization for, classified joint publications must be in accordance with DOD Manual 5200.01, Volume 1, *DOD Information Security Program: Overview, Classification, and Declassification,* and DOD Manual 5200.01, Volume 3, *DOD Information Security Program: Protection of Classified Information.*

6. Distribution of Electronic Publications

a. Joint Staff J-7 will not print copies of JPs for distribution. Electronic versions are available on JDEIS at https://jdeis.js.mil (NIPRNET) and http://jdeis.js.smil.mil (SIPRNET), and on the JEL at http://www.dtic.mil/doctrine (NIPRNET).

b. Only approved JPs and joint test publications are releasable outside the CCMDs, Services, and Joint Staff. Release of any classified JP to foreign governments or foreign nationals must be requested through the local embassy (Defense Attaché Office) to DIA, Defense Foreign Liaison/IE-3, 200 MacDill Blvd., Joint Base Anacostia-Bolling, Washington, DC 20340-5100.

c. JEL CD-ROM. Upon request of a joint doctrine development community member, the Joint Staff J-7 will produce and deliver one CD-ROM with current JPs. This JEL CD-ROM will be updated not less than semi-annually and when received can be locally reproduced for use within the CCMDs and Services.

GLOSSARY
PART I—ABBREVIATIONS AND ACRONYMS

ACM	airspace coordinating measure
AD	automatic distribution
AFWA	Air Force Weather Agency
AOI	area of interest
AOR	area of responsibility
ASG	Allied System for Geospatial Intelligence
C2	command and control
CAP	crisis action planning
CCDR	combatant commander
CCMD	combatant command
CIA	Central Intelligence Agency
CIB	controlled image base
CIL	command information library
CJCS	Chairman of the Joint Chiefs of Staff
CJCSI	Chairman of the Joint Chiefs of Staff instruction
CJCSM	Chairman of the Joint Chiefs of Staff manual
CMA	collection management authority
CNMOC	Commander, Naval Meteorology and Oceanography Command
COA	course of action
COG	center of gravity
CONOPS	concept of operations
CONPLAN	concept plan
CONUS	continental United States
COP	common operational picture
CP	control point
CSA	combat support agency
DCGS	distributed common ground/surface system
DDM	Defense Logistics Agency Distribution Mapping
DHS	Department of Homeland Security
DIA	Defense Intelligence Agency
DIGO	Defence Imagery and Geospatial Organisation (Australia)
DIJE	Defense Intelligence Joint Environment (United Kingdom)
DLA	Defense Logistics Agency
DNC	digital nautical chart
DND	Department of National Defence (Canada)
DNI	Director of National Intelligence
DOD	Department of Defense
DPPDB	digital point positioning database
DRO	departmental requirements officer
DSCA	defense support of civil authorities

DSN	Defense Switched Network
DTED	digital terrain elevation data
DVD	digital video disc
EED	emergency-essential designation
EEI	essential element of information
EGM	Earth Gravity Model
EI	environmental information
EVC	evasion chart
EXORD	execute order
FEMA	Federal Emergency Management Agency
FNMOC	Fleet Numerical Meteorology and Oceanography Center
FSCM	fire support coordination measure
FWC	fleet weather center
GA	geospatial analyst
GARS	Global Area Reference System
GBS	Global Broadcast Service
GCC	geographic combatant commander
GEOINT	geospatial intelligence
GETS	geospatial enterprise tasking, processing, exploitation, and dissemination service
GI	geomatics and imagery
GI&S	geospatial information and services
GIBCO	geospatial intelligence base for contingency operations
GIMS	Geospatial Intelligence Information Management Services
GIO	Geospatial Intelligence Organisation (New Zealand)
GPC	geospatial planning cell
GPE	geospatial intelligence preparation of the environment
GPL	Geospatial Product Library
GPS	Global Positioning System
GST	geospatial support team
HQ	headquarters
HSIP	Homeland Security Infrastructure Program
I&W	indications and warning
IA	imagery analyst
IAW	in accordance with
IBS	integrated broadcast service
IC	intelligence community
ICM	image city map
IDP	imagery derived product
IMINT	imagery intelligence
INS	inertial navigation system

IP	initial point
IPR	in-progress review
ISR	intelligence, surveillance, and reconnaissance
IT	information technology
J-2	intelligence directorate of a joint staff
J-3	operations directorate of a joint staff
J-4	logistics directorate of a joint staff
J-6	communications system directorate of a joint staff
J-7	Joint Staff Directorate for Joint Force Development
JCC	joint collaboration cell
JFC	joint force commander
JFCC	joint functional component command
JIOC	joint intelligence operations center
JIPOE	joint intelligence preparation of the operational environment
JMO	joint meteorological and oceanographic officer
JOA	joint operations area
JOG	joint operations graphic
JP	joint publication
JSCP	Joint Strategic Capabilities Plan
JTF	joint task force
JWICS	Joint Worldwide Intelligence Communications System
MAGTF	Marine air-ground task force
MASINT	measurement and signature intelligence
MCIA	Marine Corps Intelligence Activity
MCO	Mapping Customer Operations (DLA)
METOC	meteorological and oceanographic
MGRS	military grid reference system
MOD	ministry of defense
MSO	map support office
NAD 83	North American Datum 1983
NASIC	National Air and Space Intelligence Center
NAVOCEANO	Naval Oceanographic Office
NCDC	National Climatic Data Center
NGA	National Geospatial-Intelligence Agency
NIL	National Information Library
NIPRNET	Nonsecure Internet Protocol Router Network
NIST	national intelligence support team
NOAA	National Oceanic and Atmospheric Administration
NRO	National Reconnaissance Office
NSA	National Security Agency
NSG	National System for Geospatial Intelligence
NST	National Geospatial-Intelligence Agency support team

OPLAN	operation plan
OPORD	operation order
OWS	operational weather squadron
POC	point of contact
PRISM	Planning Tool for Resource, Integration, Synchronization, and Management
RGS	remote geospatial intelligence services
SA	situational awareness
SARDOT	search and rescue point
SecDef	Secretary of Defense
SIGINT	signals intelligence
SIPRNET	SECRET Internet Protocol Router Network
SMO	senior meteorological and oceanographic officer
SOF	special operations forces
2-D	two-dimensional
3-D	three-dimensional
TLM	topographic line map
TPED	tasking, processing, exploitation, and dissemination
TPFDD	time-phased force and deployment data
UGO	unified geospatial-intelligence operations
UK	United Kingdom
USA	United States Army
USAF	United States Air Force
USAFRICOM	United States Africa Command
USC	United States Code
USCENTCOM	United States Central Command
USCG	United States Coast Guard
USD(I)	Under Secretary of Defense for Intelligence
USEUCOM	United States European Command
USG	United States Government
USGS	United States Geological Survey
USMC	United States Marine Corps
USNORTHCOM	United States Northern Command
USPACOM	United States Pacific Command
USSOCOM	United States Special Operations Command
USSOUTHCOM	United States Southern Command
USSTRATCOM	United States Strategic Command
USTRANSCOM	United States Transportation Command
WARP	web-based access and retrieval portal
WGS 84	World Geodetic System 1984

WRS	war reserve stock
WS	weather squadron

advanced geospatial intelligence. None. (Approved for removal from JP 1-02.)

aeronautical chart. A specialized representation of mapped features of the Earth, or some part of it, produced to show selected terrain, cultural and hydrographic features, and supplemental information required for air navigation, pilotage, or for planning air operations. (Approved for incorporation into JP 1-02 with JP 2-03 as the source JP.)

annotation. None. (Approved for removal from JP 1-02.)

azimuth. None. (Approved for removal from JP 1-02.)

base line. None. (Approved for removal from JP 1-02.)

change detection. An image enhancement technique that compares two images of the same area from different time periods and eliminates identical picture elements in order to leave the signatures that have undergone change. (Approved for incorporation into JP 1-02.)

chart sheet. None. (Approved for removal from JP 1-02.)

combat chart. A special naval chart, at a scale of 1:50,000, designed for naval surface fire support and close air support during coastal or amphibious operations and showing detailed hydrography and topography in the coastal belt. (Approved for incorporation into JP 1-02 with JP 2-03 as the source JP.)

control. 1. Authority that may be less than full command exercised by a commander over part of the activities of subordinate or other organizations. (JP 1) 2. In mapping, charting, and photogrammetry, a collective term for a system of marks or objects on the Earth or on a map or a photograph, whose positions or elevations (or both) have been or will be determined. (JP 2-03) 3. Physical or psychological pressures exerted with the intent to assure that an agent or group will respond as directed. (JP 3-0) 4. An indicator governing the distribution and use of documents, information, or material. Such indicators are the subject of intelligence community agreement and are specifically defined in appropriate regulations. (JP 1-02. SOURCE: JP 2-01)

convergence. None. (Approved for removal from JP 1-02.)

coordinates. None. (Approved for removal from JP 1-02.)

datum (geodetic). 1. A reference surface consisting of five quantities: the latitude and longitude of an initial point, the azimuth of a line from that point, and the parameters of the reference ellipsoid. 2. The mathematical model of the earth used to calculate the coordinates on any map. Different nations use different datum for printing coordinates on their maps. (Approved for incorporation into JP 1-02.)

directional gyro indicator. None. (Approved for removal from JP 1-02.)

electronic imagery dissemination. None. (Approved for removal from JP 1-02.)

electro-optics. None. (Approved for removal from JP 1-02.)

foundation geospatial-intelligence data. The base underlying data to provide context and a framework for display and visualization of the environment to support analysis operations and intelligence, which consists of: features; elevation; controlled imagery; geodetic sciences; geographic names and boundaries; aeronautical, maritime and human geography. (Approved for replacement of "foundation data" and its definition in JP 1-02.)

gap (imagery). None. (Approved for removal from JP 1-02.)

geographic coordinates. The quantities of latitude and longitude which define the position of a point on the surface of the Earth with respect to the reference spheroid. (JP 1-02. SOURCE: JP 2-03)

geographic reference points. None. (Approved for removal from JP 1-02.)

geospatial information. Information that identifies the geographic location and characteristics of natural or constructed features and boundaries on the Earth, including: statistical data and information derived from, among other things, remote sensing, mapping, and surveying technologies; and mapping, charting, geodetic data and related products. (JP 1-02. SOURCE: JP 2-03)

geospatial information and services. The collection, information extraction, storage, dissemination, and exploitation of geodetic, geomagnetic, imagery, gravimetric, aeronautical, topographic, hydrographic, littoral, cultural, and toponymic data accurately referenced to a precise location on the Earth's surface. Also called **GI&S**. (Approved for incorporation into JP 1-02.)

geospatial intelligence. The exploitation and analysis of imagery and geospatial information to describe, assess, and visually depict physical features and geographically referenced activities on the Earth. Geospatial intelligence consists of imagery, imagery intelligence, and geospatial information. Also called **GEOINT.** (JP 1-02. SOURCE: JP 2-03)

geospatial intelligence operations. The tasks, activities, and events to collect, manage, analyze, generate, visualize, and provide imagery, imagery intelligence, and geospatial information necessary to support national and defense missions and international arrangements. Also called **GEOINT operations.** (Approved for inclusion in JP 1-02.)

grid. None. (Approved for removal from JP 1-02.)

grid bearing. None. (Approved for removal from JP 1-02.)

grid convergence. None. (Approved for removal from JP 1-02.)

grid convergence factor. None. (Approved for removal from JP 1-02.)

grid coordinate system. None. (Approved for removal from JP 1-02.)

ground control. None. (Approved for removal from JP 1-02.)

hyperspectral imagery. Term used to describe the imagery derived from subdividing the electromagnetic spectrum into very narrow bandwidths allowing images useful in precise terrain or target analysis to be formed. Also called **HSI.** (Approved for incorporation into JP 1-02.)

imagery. A likeness or presentation of any natural or man-made feature or related object or activity, and the positional data acquired at the same time the likeness or representation was acquired, including: products produced by space-based national intelligence reconnaissance systems; and likeness and presentations produced by satellites, airborne platforms, unmanned aerial vehicles, or other similar means (except that such term does not include handheld or clandestine photography taken by or on behalf of human intelligence collection organizations). (JP 1-02. SOURCE: JP 2-03)

imagery exploitation. The cycle of processing, using, interpreting, mensuration and/or manipulating imagery, and any assembly or consolidation of the results for dissemination. (Approved for incorporation into JP 1-02.)

imagery intelligence. The technical, geographic, and intelligence information derived through the interpretation or analysis of imagery and collateral materials. Also called **IMINT.** (JP 1-02. SOURCE: JP 2-03)

infrared imagery. That imagery produced as a result of sensing electromagnetic radiations emitted or reflected from a given target surface in the infrared portion of the electromagnetic spectrum (approximately 0.72 to 1,000 microns). (Approved for incorporation into JP 1-02 with JP 2-03 as the source JP.)

large-scale map. None. (Approved for removal from JP 1-02.)

map chart. None. (Approved for removal from JP 1-02.)

map sheet. None. (Approved for removal from JP 1-02.)

medium-scale map. None. (Approved for removal from JP 1-02.)

mission specific data sets. None. (Approved for removal from JP 1-02.)

National System for Geospatial Intelligence. The combination of technology, policies, capabilities, doctrine, activities, people, data, and organizations necessary to produce geospatial intelligence in an integrated, multi-intelligence environment. Also called **NSG.** (Approved for incorporation into JP 1-02.)

photomap. None. (Approved for removal from JP 1-02.)

pictomap. None. (Approved for removal from JP 1-02.)

planning factors database. Databases created and maintained by the Services for the purpose of identifying all geospatial information and services requirements for emerging and existing forces and systems. Also called **PFDB.** (Approved for incorporation into JP 1-02.)

pre-positioned war reserve requirement. None. (Approved for removal from JP 1-02.)

public key infrastructure. An enterprise-wide service that supports digital signatures and other public key-based security mechanisms for Department of Defense functional enterprise programs, including generation, production, distribution, control, and accounting of public key certificates. Also called **PKI.** (Approved for incorporation into JP 1-02.)

radar imagery. None. (Approved for removal from JP 1-02.)

radio detection. None. (Approved for removal from JP 1-02.)

secondary imagery dissemination. None. (Approved for removal from JP 1-02.)

slant range. None. (Approved for removal from JP 1-02.)

small-scale map. None. (Approved for removal from JP 1-02.)

tactical map. None. (Approved for removal from JP 1-02.)

technical analysis. In imagery interpretation, the precise description of details appearing on imagery. (Approved for incorporation into JP 1-02 with JP 2-03 as the source JP.)

temperature gradient. None. (Approved for removal from JP 1-02.)

terrain analysis. The collection, analysis, evaluation, and interpretation of geographic information on the natural and man-made features of the terrain, combined with other relevant factors, to predict the effect of the terrain on military operations. (Approved for incorporation into JP 1-02.)

thermal imagery. None. (Approved for removal from JP 1-02.)

topographic map. A map that presents the vertical position of features in measurable form as well as their horizontal positions. (Approved for inclusion in JP 1-02.)

universal polar stereographic grid. A military grid prescribed for joint use in operations in limited areas and used for operations requiring precise position reporting. It covers areas between the 80 degree parallels and the poles. (Approved for incorporation into JP 1-02 with JP 2-03 as the source JP.)

variation. None. (Approved for removal from JP 1-02.)

war reserve stock. That portion of total materiel assets designated to satisfy the war reserve materiel requirement. Also called **WRS.** (JP 1-02. SOURCE: JP 2-03)

JOINT DOCTRINE PUBLICATIONS HIERARCHY

JP 1
JOINT DOCTRINE
JP 1-0
PERSONNEL
JP 2-0
INTELLIGENCE
JP 3-0
OPERATIONS
JP 4-0
LOGISTICS
JP 5-0
PLANS
JP 6-0
COMMUNICATIONS SYSTEM

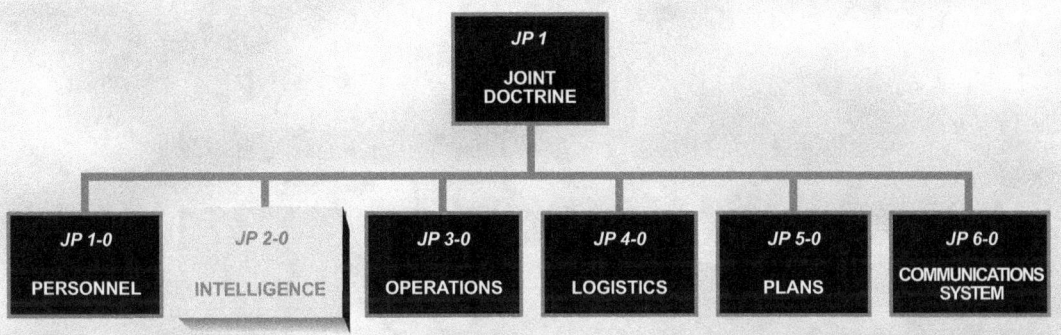

All joint publications are organized into a comprehensive hierarchy as shown in the chart above. **Joint Publication (JP) 2-03** is in the **Intelligence** series of joint doctrine publications. The diagram below illustrates an overview of the development process:

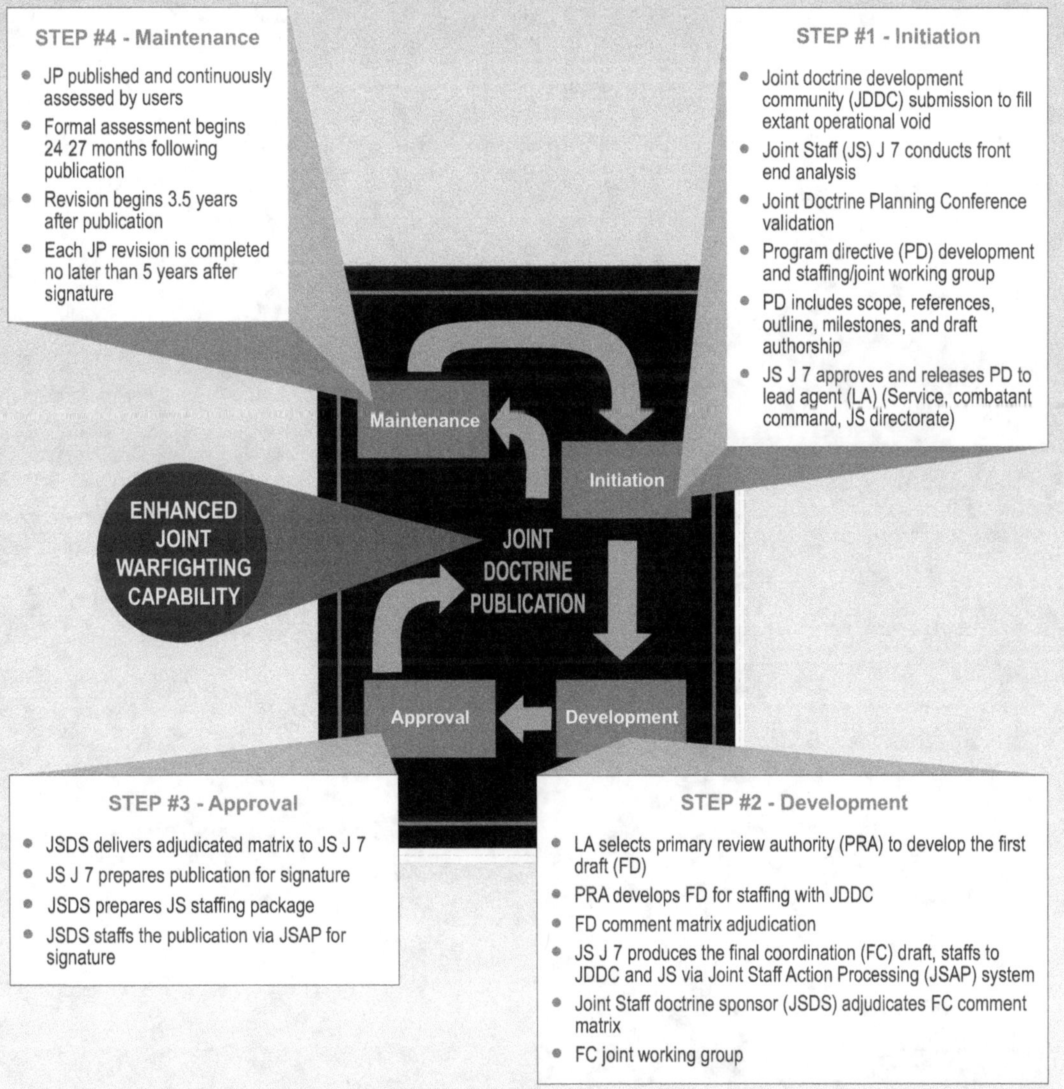

STEP #4 - Maintenance
JP published and continuously assessed by users
Formal assessment begins 24 27 months following publication
Revision begins 3.5 years after publication
Each JP revision is completed no later than 5 years after signature
STEP #1 - Initiation
Joint doctrine development community (JDDC) submission to fill extant operational void
Joint Staff (JS) J 7 conducts front end analysis
Joint Doctrine Planning Conference validation
Program directive (PD) development and staffing/joint working group
PD includes scope, references, outline, milestones, and draft authorship
JS J 7 approves and releases PD to lead agent (LA) (Service, combatant command, JS directorate)
Maintenance
Initiation
ENHANCED JOINT WARFIGHTING CAPABILITY
JOINT DOCTRINE PUBLICATION
Approval
Development
STEP #3 - Approval
JSDS delivers adjudicated matrix to JS J 7
JS J 7 prepares publication for signature
JSDS prepares JS staffing package
JSDS staffs the publication via JSAP for signature
STEP #2 - Development
LA selects primary review authority (PRA) to develop the first draft (FD)
PRA develops FD for staffing with JDDC
FD comment matrix adjudication
JS J 7 produces the final coordination (FC) draft, staffs to JDDC and JS via Joint Staff Action Processing (JSAP) system
Joint Staff doctrine sponsor (JSDS) adjudicates FC comment matrix
FC joint working group

www.ingramcontent.com/pod-product-compliance
Lightning Source LLC
Chambersburg PA
CBHW081326310526
45789CB00018B/2407